to be more crucial to Bluebell selection than being a polished dancer. As Phillips observes, "[G]irls over five-foot-eight weren't a dime a dozen in post-war England."

For seven months–from 1960 through 1961–Phillips toured Italy with a Bluebell troupe as part of a musical comedy/variety show extravaganza, the *Dapporto Spettacolo*, which traveled to 52 cities and towns. The cast rehearsed and performed daily, and sometimes did both twice a day, seven days a week. Finding time to date was difficult. This led to forbidden relationships between dancers and roadshow staff, many of whom were married. Phillips avoided this complication, in part, by becoming a prolific letter writer to family and boyfriend. Decades later, the letters helped in writing her book, *HAVE CHIGNON - WILL TRAVEL*, which isn't dramatic but is rich in detail. No doubt the correspondence aided recollection of exhausting experiences such as the final month of the tour, which Phillips likened to a series of "one-night stands" as the cast rushed from one town to the next with almost no time for sleep or sightseeing. Bluebell life was literally costly because the pressure on dancers to look chic was constant. They were expected to pay for tailored clothing and trips to beauty parlors (chignons were a favorite style). They also had to cover lodging, meals, and train fare. Although Phillips makes it clear that she loved her sojourn on stage, she chose to quit the chorus line for a different adventure, which is also detailed in her book. Her memoir is a worthy choice for anyone fascinated by theater and dance history.

HAVE CHIGNON - WILL TRAVEL is Elizabeth Dale Phillips' richly detailed memoir about the touring life of a showgirl in the early 1960s and is a worthy choice for anyone fascinated by theater and dance history. *–**IndieReader Review***

"I was going to Italy on the following Monday! I was going to be a Bluebell Girl!"

Elizabeth was weeks away from graduation, on the precipice of youth and adulthood. Options for women were limited to being a wife and mother or a secretary until married. Her family was already astonished at her courageous move to London immediately after receiving her diploma. She was happy with her newly found independence, and providing for herself gave her self-confidence. Still, she felt as though she was seeking something more.

When Elizabeth's mom encouraged her to try out for the Bluebells, she was exhilarated and scared. The Bluebells were the definition of glamour and excitement in Europe during the fifties and sixties. To be a Bluebell was to be in an exclusive sorority. Elizabeth auditioned several times before getting invited to dance in Italy. No one in her family had ever left the country. The next year was a whirlwind of practices and performances in cities all over Italy and France. Although the dancers were overwhelmed with their duties, there was occasionally time to explore their surroundings and enjoy the culture. Elizabeth learned a lot about people and herself living in this microcosm of a performance troupe. Upon returning home to Birmingham, she felt much changed and ready for life's next adventure.

This memoir, an action-packed journey through Italy and France, is based on hundreds of letters written to and from the author while she was overseas. She wrote the book in her eighties, nearly six decades after dancing with the troupe. This offers both the firsthand account as she experienced it in her youth and the perspective gained from maturity. The reader is treated to a behind-the-scenes glimpse of the dedication, glamour, and drama of a dance company.

Imaginations will be captivated by vivid descriptions of Italian towns and extraordinary theatres. The author has created an exciting, endearing, and delightful memoir.
—**Gretchen Hansen, *US Review of Books***

Phillips's immersive memoir relates in impressive detail what it was like to be a member of the dance troupe The Bluebell Girls, traveling through Italy in the early 1960s. Growing up in Birmingham, England, Phillips knew that an ultimate honor for a dancer was to become a Bluebell. She shares the details of this journey starting from her first audition, when was told she was what they were looking for but had several things to learn first, and then the many hours of work she put in—all while working a day job—to finally be offered a contract to tour Italy. Phillips then brings readers through each stop of the nine-month tour with the storied troupe, a remarkable time where every bit of fun met exceptionally hard work.

To contemporary readers, much of what the Bluebells were required to do on a daily basis will be surprising, and a great departure from what an employer could ask of employees now. Miss Bluebell and the troupe captain, Vera, not only dictated how each danced or looked on stage, but also how to look, act, and even who they could associate with outside the theater. They were not allowed to leave the theater or hotel they were staying in without makeup and hair done, representing the Bluebells at all times. Phillips herself was also told to turn her hair blonde and straighten it nightly with uncomfortable rollers.

While frequently annoyed by demands of decorum—and the regular bursts of rebellion from some of the girls—they were recognized almost everywhere they went, they were often treated like royalty with many admirers and invitations to extravagant parties. Above all, their love to dance and for each other as a family shines throughout the book. From the stage to the daily worries like saving money (they were required to pay for their rooms and meals), readers will appreciate the fascinating details Phillips shares about each stop along the way.

Takeaway: An entertaining, first-hand look at life as a dancing Bluebell in 1960, touring Italy.

Great for fans of: Corliss Fyfe Whitney's *A Rockette Remembers: Tales from a High Kicking Life*, Toni Bentley's *Winter Season*.

Production grades

Cover: A	Design and typography: A
Illustrations: A	Editing: A
Marketing copy: A	

—**BookLife - *Publishers Weekly* Review**

In her debut memoir, Phillips recounts her time touring Italy in the 1960s with the Bluebell Girls, an international dance troupe.

Growing up as a working-class teenager in post–World War II England, the author read news reports about the glamorous Bluebell Girls, an all-female dance company founded by Irishwoman Margaret Kelly that performed around the world with "star billing in long-running cabaret shows like those at the Lido in Paris and the Stardust in Las Vegas." A self-described underachiever from Birmingham, Phillips never imagined that she would become a Bluebell herself, but she soon found herself in the running thanks in part to her love of theater and her height (Bluebells were required to be taller than 5 feet, 8 inches). Despite minimal dance training, Phillips was awarded a nine-month contract to tour Italy with the *Dapporto Spettacolo*, a star-vehicle show featuring Italian actor

Carlo Dapporto. Phillips chronicles the excitement, triumphs, mishaps, and hardships of being a touring dancer in a foreign country, complete with onstage and backstage drama. She describes the exacting, expensive standards that Bluebells were expected to uphold and her dramatic transformation from a "frizzy-haired shorthand typist" to a world-traveling sophisticate. Overseeing every aspect of the girls' public image and personal lives was an overbearing dance captain, Vera, who frequently butted heads with Phillips' fellow Bluebells, musicians, technicians, and eager Italian paramours. Throughout, the author recounts the beautiful sights and unfamiliar customs of the Italian countryside as well as the grueling aspects of her days as a dancer: "It wasn't unusual for our daily quota of sleep to be split into two or three segments." All the while, she narrates her story with an approachable tone of fond remembrance. She's rarely judgmental and always seeking to contextualize the experience of being a young, female performer in Italy in the 1960s. Although Phillips' memoir feels less like a structured narrative and more like a stream-of-consciousness yarn, her anecdotes are entertaining and will no doubt intrigue lovers of dance and theater.

A pleasing memoir and an enlightening glimpse into the Bluebell Girls experience. *—**Kirkus Reviews***

HAVE CHIGNON
–WILL TRAVEL

HAVE CHIGNON –WILL TRAVEL

TOURING ITALY WITH THE BLUEBELL GIRLS 1960-61

ELIZABETH DALE PHILLIPS

W. Brand Publishing
NASHVILLE, TENNESSEE

Permission granted by Reach Publishing to use *Daily Express* and *Daily Mirror* excerpts.

Permission granted by Alfred Music to use excerpt from *Kiss Me Kate*.

j.brand@wbrandpub.com
W. Brand Publishing
www.wbrandpub.com

Cover design by JuLee Brand / designchik.net
Cover photo credit: Elio Luxardo
The Luxardo Family has kindly granted permission for The Bluebell Girls portrait by Elio Luxardo to be used as the cover of this book.

Have Chignon—Will Travel / Elizabeth Dale Phillips —1st ed.

Available in Paperback, Kindle, and eBook formats.
Hardcover ISBN: 978-1-950385-75-1
Paperback ISBN: 978-1-950385-63-8
eBook ISBN: 978-1-950385-64-5

Library of Congress Control Number: 2021910379

CONTENTS

ACKNOWLEDGEMENTS

My biggest thank-you goes to my daughter-in-law Frances Key Phillips. A couple of years ago, my husband and I were visiting our family in Connecticut, and I was standing around the kitchen while she cooked, and telling her about my current project: transcribing dozens and dozens of letters I'd written sixty years ago, when I was a dancer touring Italy—I wanted them in a readable form so my children and grandchildren could enjoy them. She asked a few questions and I started to tell her about the life I'd led: the glamour, the one-night stands, the scrapes, and the characters I'd been surrounded by.

She stopped her cooking, looked up at me, and said, "There's a story there." And here's the wonderful part: Frances is a book editor and she offered, there and then, that if I wrote the book, she would edit it. For a first time writer, life can't get much better than that. So, I wrote the book and, true to her word, Frances has guided me through the task of transforming 104,000 words of raw anecdotes into an interesting story. Thank you, Frances.

Next, a big thank you to JuLee Brand, who took my story, performed her magic, and produced a book.

And, many thanks to my husband, Bill. He's been the "first and last eyes" on my work and my biggest supporter, who always made sure that I had a comfortable spot in the house in which to work, and always encouraged me to "get back to writing."

And lastly, thank you to all those friends and family members who motivated me with "how's the book coming." I can't wait to tell them that it's finished.

For my granddaughter
Alexandra

and

all the Bluebell Girls
who went before and since
and, in particular,
those I worked with in the
Dapporto Spettacolo 1960-61

AUTHOR'S NOTE

These are my memories, assisted by the many letters I wrote at the time. I fully recognize that others will have both experienced and remembered events differently. Some names have been changed to protect their privacy.

With affection for my fellow Bluebells,
Elizabeth
2021

CHAPTER ONE

SO YOU WANT TO BE A BLUEBELL

In the 1950s and '60s The Bluebell Girls, troupes of young dancers, were renowned throughout Europe and further afield. As a teenager in England, I'd read stories of newly hired "Bluebells" in my local paper, the *Birmingham Mail,* and in the national tabloids; I'd read interviews with Miss Bluebell, and I'd seen a photograph of Bluebells standing at the bottom of airplane stairs, newly arrived in Las Vegas, newsworthy because they were the first Bluebell Girls to dance in the U.S.

The Bluebell Girls were named for their director, Margaret Kelly, known to all as "Miss Bluebell." (As a baby she had incredibly blue eyes; a doctor commented on this, and from that day she was "Bluebell.") The majority of the dancers were English and there were about five troupes working around the world at any one time, in such places as Lucerne, Stockholm, Cannes, Buenos Aires, Tokyo, Italy, Geneva, Barcelona, and a weekly TV show in Rome. In addition, they had star billing in long-running cabaret shows like those at the Lido in Paris and the Stardust in Las Vegas.

Bluebell Girls appeared to lead extraordinary lives. They were known to be highly paid, wear gorgeous costumes on-stage, and be fashionably dressed off-stage. Much of their appeal derived from their statuesque appearance. They were all exceptionally tall, an impression enhanced on-stage by three-inch heels, four-inch-high chignons and costumes that were cut away at the thighs to further elongate their legs.

An article in the *Daily Express* in 1963 introduced Julie, a newly hired Bluebell Girl:

> *Julie, who trained at ballet school and comes from Crystal Palace, has been after a job with the Bluebells since she was 13.*
>
> *Recently Miss Bluebell arranged to have Julie's teeth straightened* (nothing but perfection will do) ... *and now she has got the job, the* only *present vacancy among the 100 Bluebell Girls dancing in troupes in Paris, Rome, Milan, Las Vegas and Tokyo.*
>
> *For getting into the Bluebell line-up is as easy as getting on the board of I.C.I.* (the largest publicly held company in the UK at the time). *And the rewards are about as great.*
>
> *Peter Baker, the Bluebell business manager, showed me a list of savings sent home after one month's work by the girls in Tokyo. Most were over £100* (well over $1000 in 2020).
>
> *Said Miss Bluebell: "They deserve the reward. They work hard and they give pleasure to people, so why not. Most of the girls in Las Vegas have their own cars and small houses. And I've never had to get rid of a girl for age reasons, most get married ... and very good marriages, too."*
>
> *"Why the great success?" Said Miss Bluebell, "I suppose it's mainly because I know how to pick the girls. We don't just look for height. They have to be good dancers ... they have all*

*trained in ballet . . . they have to be very attractive, and they must
have good backgrounds." Said Mr. Baker, "I think one of the se-
crets is that the girls are all perfect when they go on stage. Lipstick,
eyes, hairdo, dress. Nothing less than perfect allowed.*

When that article was written, only one in twenty young
people in England went on to higher education, and the majority of young women looked forward only to a dead-end job,
for which short-hand and typing skills were the requirements,
and which would fill the few years until they were "rescued"
by marriage and children. The thought of living the life of a
Bluebell Girl never entered their consciousness. It was completely outside the realm of possibility.

Like most girls in England, it never crossed my mind that I
could be a Bluebell Girl. When I was in high school, I'd been
involved in theatrical and musical activities. They were the
only areas in which I shone. Any excuse, I could be found on
the stage. Academically I wasn't as successful, largely because
I didn't work, my report cards always ending with "Elizabeth
could do better if she applied herself." As "applying myself"
didn't sound like much fun and required me to understand
the concept of long-term goals, I never did "do better." But
things weren't completely hopeless, as by the time I left school
in July 1958, I'd been accepted at the Preparatory School of
the Royal Academy of Dramatic Art (RADA) in London, a
prep school that had been established to prepare young actors
for the highly competitive audition for acceptance at RADA.
(Today, the school no longer exists.)

Later that summer I received a letter from the school stating
that they could no longer offer me a place. No explanation was

given, and we never sought one. The news came as a shock to my family, who had been set to enjoy my future in the theater. My mother, so disappointed that this opportunity had been snatched away from me, sat down and cried; the first time I'd ever seen her cry. Now, looking back, I realize she only wanted me to have opportunities that she hadn't had when she was young, so she had every reason to be disappointed. Anyway, the moment passed. I was shocked, but I didn't cry. I, too, was disappointed but also relieved, as I had no idea how my parents were going to pay the fees. I'd heard whispers hinting they were planning on borrowing from one of my godmothers which, although I wasn't familiar with the family's finances, I recognized as a bad plan. I was well aware that, in that era, acting jobs were few and far between, so instead of feeling heartbroken, I felt that fate had probably done me a favor. The original acceptance to the school had been sufficient for my teenage ego, allowing me to enjoy the last months of high school with a slightly more glamorous post-high school plan than any of my friends.

That summer I started work in a sewing-notions shop in Birmingham, still living with my parents. With my new earnings, around £3.15 a week, I returned to the acting teacher who I'd worked with prior to the RADA-Prep School audition, as I was now preparing directly for the RADA audition. My teacher was well known in the Midlands because during the war he'd directed a female vocal group, The Arden Singers, who performed for British and Allied servicemen, hospitals, at munition factories and such, with songs, drama, and poetry readings.

He envisioned me developing into a performer similar to the comedian Joyce Grenfell. That seemed to be aiming rather high, but I followed his direction when he advised me to add dance to my current theater skills, and I began taking modern dance and tap lessons at the Betty Fox Stage School.

The Betty Fox Stage School was well known in the Midlands because not only was it a dance school, it was also a theatrical agency. As such it provided the chorus lines for variety shows, and for the many pantomimes that were produced each Christmas season in towns and cities around England. After a few weeks of lessons, Betty Fox herself offered me a job in *Jack and Jill*, a pantomime starring the comedian Charlie Chester, to be produced in Hanley, north of Birmingham, in the Potteries. I wasn't being hired as a dancer, however, but as a singer. Two members of the chorus were to be the understudies for the Principal Boy and Principal Girl, and I was to be the latter. When not fulfilling our understudy role, when all twelve girls were singing, our voices would add body to the sound, and when the other ten girls danced, we singers were to stand around the stage, giving appropriate nods and smiles at whatever was happening adjacent to us.

Pantomimes traditionally open on Boxing Day, December 26, and rehearsals for our chorus began on December 17. After one day the choreographer told us two singers that we looked awkward standing at the edge of the stage, and that we should learn all the dances. We did. Where possible we were placed in the back row, so as not to "let the side down" with our relative lack of skill, but sometimes there was no avoiding it.

In one particular number where we were all dressed as kitchen maids, we formed a single line across the front of the stage. In each hand we held two spoons, joined together like large sugar tongs, and we manipulated them, clacking them together, sounding like castanets. It was a clever idea, fun and easily mastered. We wore tap shoes for this number which was treacherous for a non-dancer. I never did learn to tap dance, but I did learn to fake it, always praying I wouldn't tap a solitary 'tap' during a beat of silence.

I loved appearing in *Jack and Jill*. The professional production was so much more enjoyable than the school sponsored efforts I had experienced up until then. At school, fellow performers had been allowed to skip rehearsals if they had a conflicting activity, such as a sports event. Not so in the professional theater, not if you wanted to keep your job. It was such a different atmosphere; the finished product mattered to everyone.

It all came to an end in mid-February, and the next eighteen months were not my happiest. First, I tried, unsuccessfully, to get a job in a vocal chorus of an ice show. This was followed by a period of unemployment, then a seven-month stint in a photography lab, and finally, realizing I needed a skill, I completed a shorthand-typing course. Newly employable, I joined a friend in a flat in London.

I'd been in London around four months when, finding myself dejected following failed attempts to rekindle a past relationship, I needed cheering up. My mother, wanting to see me occupied by something other than thoughts of a young man who wasn't worthy of me, came up with just the thing. She sent me an article from the *Birmingham Mail*, similar to the one quoted previously, featuring a local girl who had recently been hired as a Bluebell Girl. Miss Bluebell, according to the article, was always looking for girls who were "5' 8" or taller with dance experience." Wasn't that me? I certainly had "dance experience"—nine whole weeks of it—and I was definitely over 5'8".

Interested parties could contact Peter Baker, the article advised, and within a few days I had visited his apartment, demonstrated my kicks and a combination of dance steps, and was given instructions to attend the next Bluebell Girls auditions, to be held in London the following week. There I would meet Miss Bluebell, who lived in Paris and visited London every few months to hold auditions.

The audition was held in Soho, in Mac's Rehearsal Rooms, located in the basement of a building opposite the Windmill Theater. The audition hours were noon to 3 p.m. I went at noon, so as to use my lunch hour and not take time off from my job. When I walked in, I was nervous. This was an improbable situation for me to find myself in: an audition for the most desirable show-dancer job in Europe. Not only that, I was about to meet Miss Bluebell in the flesh.

When I arrived, there weren't many girls waiting, and I made it known to Peter Baker that I was on my lunch-hour, so I was glad when I didn't have to wait around very long before Miss Bluebell talked to me. I was immediately impressed: she was an attractive woman, of medium height, good figure, had short neatly styled hair and was elegantly dressed. She was very personable, yet radiated authority over those around her, including Peter Baker and us would-be Bluebells.

7

She immediately asked me about my dancing experience, and I gave her every last detail of my experience at the Betty Fox Stage School, the dance requirements of *Jack and Jill* and the short stint I'd had with a second dance studio later that year, including details of the Cossack Dance I'd performed in a studio recital.

She asked me to demonstrate kicks and *pirouettes*, and then showed me a very simple combination of steps that I should perform. I followed every instruction she gave me and then waited for the verdict.

She began with some compliments, such as, "You are just what I'm looking for." Having heard that, it was easy not to be too discouraged when I heard her next words, which were "but you can't dance." And then she continued—she wanted me to go away and work very hard, and she would see me again at a future audition. That was the end of the audition, and I was directed to talk to Peter Baker, who was to give me the specifics regarding how I was to "work very hard."

I'd just been rejected but felt fine about it. It seemed that she was looking for other attributes in addition to the ability to dance, a certain look, perhaps. And evidently, she was satisfied that I had it.

Peter Baker immediately took me in hand instructing me to attend ballet classes at a studio off Cambridge Circus three evenings a week, and to stay in touch. I followed his instructions, even adding a Saturday morning class to the schedule, never missing a class for the following six or so months, diligently working on my *rond de jambe par terre* and my *pas de chat*, and everything in between. Even though what I learned in those classes didn't make up for the years of ballet training I'd missed, my body became more limber, and I learned to move my arms, legs, torso, and head with more grace.

The ballet classes were a wonderful experience. All the attendees were out-of-work dancers keeping themselves in shape and ready for their next audition. The teacher, who we called *Madame*, and the other dancers were encouraging and never belittling—there were even hints of envy toward me and another Peter Baker protégé, Joan, with our 5'8"-plus height; in the dancing world, they told us, if you were tall, you were never out of work.

Around May, Joan was missing from class, and *Madame* told me she'd heard from her, and that she was now working at the Lido in Paris. I was slightly envious, but not despondent. Yes, she had some advantages over me, she was taller, had a body more willing to move like a ballet dancer, but had been taking classes longer than me, so I was certain my day would come, and I'd be selected. Imagine my surprise when a few weeks later Joan appeared at class, in street clothes. She had quit her job at the Lido. She didn't like the life in Paris, and her fiancé wanted her back in England. Then I learned that she'd been hired as a showgirl, not as a dancer. I was aware that the shows at the Lido and Stardust had showgirls, (girls who wore sumptuous costumes and headdresses, but with breasts uncovered) but hadn't, for one moment, thought that that was what Peter Baker was grooming us for.

That same evening, I called Peter Baker and made it very clear to him that I was only interested in being a dancer. He assured me he understood that. So, I continued ballet classes and checked in with Miss Bluebell regularly as to when she would come over to London to hold auditions.

Aspirations of being a Bluebell Girl weren't the only things on my mind that summer. In July, Ian, the brother of my friend Gill, returned home from Canada where he was a student. I was in Birmingham for the weekend when the two of them, along with my London flatmate, Ros, arrived at the door of my parent's house and asked me to join them for the evening. They were driving out of the city to a country pub. Visiting pubs, full of smoke, alcohol and noise, was not high on my preferred ways to spend an evening, but something social and unexpected rarely, if ever, happened to me, so I went. I hadn't seen Gill since the previous summer, and I hadn't seen Ian for over two years, so it was great to meet up again. The following weekend Ros and I returned to Birmingham as it was Gill's twenty-first birthday party so I saw Ian again.

Ian and I were immediately attracted to each other. It wasn't a surprise to me, and maybe not to him either. We'd known each other since I was fourteen and he was sixteen, back when we spent Saturday evenings square dancing at a church hall near his home. My parents had been very protective of their little girl, but if a social event where I could come in contact with boys was held on church premises, I was allowed to attend. So, every Saturday evening I would make the trip to Rednal with my friend, Wendy, who lived next door to my home (our families shared a semi-detach). Ian would be my only partner during the evening, and at the end he would accompany Wendy and me all the way home, as it was late for young girls to be out alone. This had been quite heroic of him: fifteen minutes on a bus and then a ten-minute walk to our houses. On one occasion Wendy wasn't there, it was just Ian and me, and when we arrived outside my house, he took the opportunity to kiss me.

In the years since, we had drifted apart but I'd stayed friendly with his family. I'd always attended their New Year's Eve parties and had remained friendly with Gill; we'd been on a vacation, with friends, in Devon the previous summer. In the meantime, Ian had attended and graduated from Birmingham University, spent two years at Queen's University in Canada, and was planning on returning there for two more years of graduate school.

For the next few weeks, while he remained in Birmingham visiting with family and friends, I saw him on the weekends. We quickly decided we wanted to see more of each other beyond these few weeks, and that when I'd saved the fare, I would visit him in Canada. We thought this would take a year; I didn't want him to subsidize the trip as I wanted to be independent.

In 1960, many British young people were emigrating, so it was not an outlandish notion, and I was thrilled with this new life-plan. I wasn't going to stop working on becoming a Bluebell Girl, but it was nice to have a back-up plan.

And while I enjoyed my few weeks of romance, back in London, in the world of auditions and dance, Miss Bluebell remained interested in me even though I could not have been her ideal candidate. Why did she remain interested in me? Certainly, girls over five-foot-eight weren't a dime a dozen in post-war England, plus I must have had other attributes that she perceived as important. I now can speculate that she thought that I would look good in stage make-up, under lights, wearing a flattering costume. Second, I was a young woman with the personality and bearing that she liked to hire, and lastly, she had evidence that I had tenacity, which boded well for my fitting into a life of hard, somewhat monotonous, work. Each time I saw her she would evaluate my progress, tell me I was "coming along nicely," and encourage me to keep up my attendance at the ballet classes. This I did.

By mid-July of that year, I was on the brink of being selected. Miss Bluebell wanted me in a new Las Vegas show and the girls, both dancers and showgirls, would be leaving soon for the States. However, there was a catch. As a prerequisite for me to join the company I had to be able to perform the splits and, an equally impossible feat, to kick my right leg as high as I could kick my left. (I assumed the Las Vegas show had a Can-Can number.) I was given one week to master these skills. Peter Baker told me that if I succeeded by the following Monday, one week later, I could sign the contract "there and then." He also warned me about a clause in the contract. "After a week of rehearsals if a girl isn't learning the dances quickly enough, she can be sent home," he said, noting that there would be only one other girl in the show who'd done as little dancing as me. He added that, "you're the sort of girl I want to send there." Seeing as I believed what I'd recently read in the *Daily Mirror*, that Miss Bluebell only wanted girls "whose morals are as lofty as their high kicks," I assumed that he was inferring that, on the "classy versus non-classy continuum," I was closer to the classy end. He also added that, once in Las Vegas, I'd probably have to "go blonde."

That week, I made countless attempts at stretching my body in ways it didn't want to stretch. Friends would push down on my shoulders, over and over again, hoping it would result in successful splits. "She must give way sometime!" they'd say. I learned all the stretching exercises routinely practiced by high-jumpers and hurdlers and, as a result, I would become looser, only to tighten up again by the next morning. As they would've said in 1960, you could "still get a double-decker bus under me!"

Even Peter Baker got in on the act, having me do back-bends, examining my spine for any hypothetical ailment he thought might be causing the deficiency. It was all to no avail. In our next phone call, Mr. Baker told me he was completing the paperwork for the work permits and passports. "Surely you can do the splits," he said impatiently, to which I admitted that I still couldn't. The next time we spoke, he was blunt. "I'm not sending you to Las Vegas because you couldn't cope with the work."

So, I didn't go to Las Vegas. I was pretty adept at recovering from, or even not registering, disappointment, so I wasn't unduly upset by this turn of events. As I didn't have a background in dance, I'd always known that getting a job in the Bluebells was a long shot. Having said that, I was still in contention for Bluebell employment, so I continued to attend ballet classes four times a week, as it was my understanding that I'd be hired by Miss Bluebell when an appropriate opening became available. Also, I was sure that I would continue to get encouragement from Peter Baker because he benefited from the current arrangement, the availability of a dancer who was ready to join a show (one where the splits and high kicks were not a prerequisite) at a moment's notice.

Meanwhile, I was having a particularly busy week. During the workday I was training my replacement at the Metal

Box Company (I'd given my notice a few weeks back), and in the evenings, after attending dance class, I was moving my belongings out of the Bayswater flat to my brother's bedsitter, also in Bayswater. (This was hard work. None of the buildings had elevators and I didn't own a car). The school year was over and my flatmates, a teacher and a couple of students, were going their separate ways and we'd given up the flat. I spent a few nights sleeping wherever I could find a bed, and finally took over the bedsitter of an acquaintance at dance class, while she was to be away on vacation. It was in Chelsea, a step up from Bayswater, so I was thrilled. She even had a coffee percolator, so, for the first time in my life I had morning coffee.

Also, during that week, Peter Baker had been in touch. Even though I wouldn't be needed for the Las Vegas contract, he let me know I should attend the Bluebell audition the following Thursday. It seemed Miss Bluebell was still interested in me.

The last day on the job at Metal Box arrived. To send me on my way, they gave me a manicure set and an ash tray; what every girl needed in 1960! The following Monday I started a "temp" job in a solicitor's office. Monday evening, I arrived back at my new Chelsea digs after spending a few hours with my brother to find a phone message from Peter Baker. "Call me immediately." I did. I was going to Italy on the following Monday! I was going to be a Bluebell Girl! (Details to be finalized at the audition.)

I was beside myself with excitement. Not only being selected as a Bluebell Girl, but going abroad for the first time, and not just abroad, *Italy*! Could there be anything more wonderful to happen to a person?! I would be the first person in my family to ever step outside of England, other than as a guest of the British Army. On every level it was a monumental occurrence!

There was a big problem. I needed a passport and there were many steps to getting one and few were simple or fast. First, I needed an application that could only be obtained from the Labor Exchange. Working around the hours of my job, it took me two visits to obtain the application, and completely used up Tuesday, and I needed to have the passport issued on Friday at the latest. Once I had the form, I could see what documents were needed. First, the easy things were accomplished: a trip to a travel agent to have my photograph taken, which I'd be picking up the following day, and a lunchtime visit with my brother for a loan to cover the fee.

I needed my birth certificate and my father's written permission. My mother gathered these, managed to catch the 8 p.m. mail in Birmingham, and I received the documents the following day, Thursday. Also, the application needed a cosigner, a person who'd known me for two years, who wasn't a personal friend and was a "member of a recognized profession or a person of good standing in their community." A list of professions was given that could only have been dreamed up by the English and ranged from chiropodist to Member of Parliament and excluded all trades. Here I had a problem as I'd not been in London for two years so would need to find someone in Birmingham. I put off solving this problem until I saw Peter Baker at the audition on Thursday as I was optimistic that he could fix it for me. The passport office also needed to see my Bluebell contract which I would also receive on Thursday when I met Miss Bluebell.

Peter Baker had told me to "look glam" for this final audition, stressing multiple times that I *had* to do "something about" my hair, which meant a trip to the hairdresser on Thursday morning—as though I didn't have enough things to do that day! He then asked me about the old and faded leotard I always wore to auditions. I explained that, although I owned three leotards, that was the only one with cut-away legs (cut away to make my legs appear longer). I'd "have to cut away the legs of one of the other leotards," he said.

On the day of the audition, I had my hair "shampoo'd and set," worked for a couple of hours, then went to my meeting with Miss Bluebell. As at previous auditions, she asked me a few questions then she demonstrated a step combination for me to perform, and I had no problems accomplishing this. However, I was there to receive a contract and there was a hitch. Contracts had two copies, one for Miss Bluebell and one for the dancer. She had one complete contract with her and one contract where one of the pages was missing. She said to me, "I'm using the complete contract for another girl, who has to get back to Sheffield today. Come to my hotel this evening and I'll have your contract waiting for you."

While I waited for the girl from Sheffield to be sent on her way, I sat around with a slender, not too tall, middle-aged American, from New York. He was to be the choreographer of "my" Italian show. He showed no interest in me, while I asked him some rudimentary questions about the States. Little did I know what an important part of my life he would become for the next five weeks!

Peter Baker was there, of course, and told me to "get in touch with me this afternoon to arrange this evening's meeting." I asked him, "Can you arrange for a cosigner for my passport application?" He said, "no." Of course, it would've been highly illegal if he'd said "yes" but I couldn't think how else he thought I was going to get a passport by close-of-business on the following day. In fact, both he and Miss Bluebell were very concerned about the cosigner issue and told me "to get right on it."

Once out of the audition I hurried back to my workplace and told them I was taking the afternoon off, then immediately raced over to my brother's workplace. He was away, but his friend had offered to lend me money for an evening trip to Birmingham in search of a "professional." Our family certainly didn't know too many professionals, but several teachers lived on the same road as we lived, and the curate at the local Anglican Church visited my grandmother on a weekly basis and I'd bumped into him a few times, and he'd even asked after me once. If we couldn't find a teacher, surely he would do.

However, before taking further action I called my mother to see if she knew anyone in or near London who was a member of a profession. She immediately came up with two names with phone numbers: a physician in London and a clergyman in Hertfordshire.

I immediately called the phone number of the Wimpole Street physician and reminded him of when he'd met me at my family home. He said he'd be delighted to sign the passport application. "I'm about to leave my rooms. Can you be at the entrance to Regent's Park Tube Station in ten minutes?" (It was a good job I was young and fit. I seemed to be doing a lot of running around!) I was there, and the application was signed. Two final things before I could call it a day. Back to Piccadilly to return the loan I hadn't needed, and a phone call to my mother to let her know that all problems were resolved.

That evening I went with Peter Baker to visit Miss Bluebell in her hotel room, where I was handed one sheet of a contract that she completed and signed while I stood next to her. She didn't have a contract with a duplicate, so I never did sign a contract. I'd already learned that Miss Bluebell had a reputation for looking after her girls well, so a contract was merely a formality, necessary only for the passport office.

The show I was to appear in, the *Dapporto Spettacolo*, would rehearse in Milan and then tour Italy for eight months. I would be earning £24 a week (four times my Metal Box salary) and I couldn't change the color of my hair without receiving permission first. Before leaving, I had the forethought to ask if I would need to take money with me, and she said, "Hardly anything. I'll look after you." That was good news!

That weekend, I purchased the largest suitcase I could find, thirty inches long with expanding hinges; an early twenty-first birthday gift from my grandmother. Both my parents came to London to say goodbye to me. Before setting out from Birmingham on Saturday morning, my mother gave piano lessons, then took the train and arrived in time for us to go to the theater in the evening. My father had to man the family hardware store on Saturday, so he couldn't come until Sunday morning. He was the family cook, so he brought sandwiches he'd made for all three of us, to keep us fed all day. We weren't a family that frequented restaurants.

My mother, the family's master-packer, packed my cases, making sure to include an umbrella, fur boots (I had been told it snows in Italy), a swimsuit, and all the clothes I owned that didn't look worn. (I'd thrown those away the previous week). So, things packed included two pretty summer dresses, two winter skirts, and a washable off-white raincoat. Also, lots of books for the journey. We said our goodbyes at the train station, and they were back on their way to Birmingham.

Late that night, going over everything one last time, I checked my passport. Occupation: Ballet Dancer. I wasn't so sure about that!

And one more thing: *Where, exactly, was Milan?*

CHAPTER 2

MEETING THE BLUEBELLS

The following morning, Monday, I arrived under the clock at Victoria Station; a traditional meeting place for train travelers, particularly those who might not recognize each other. Peter Baker had told me to be there at 8:30 sharp; I was. He had also told me to "look pretty." I did my best.

Seven girls were gathered: three current Bluebells, flawlessly turned out and immaculately coiffed, three new girls, and me. It was not difficult to figure out which were which.

The current Bluebells were Carol, Deanna, and Alice, all eighteen years old. Carol and Deanna were both experienced Bluebells and had most recently been working at the Lido in Paris. Alice, who'd begun a year ago as a non-dancer like me, had recently danced in Lucerne.

The new girls were Jessie, Annie, and Sylvia. Sylvia was the oldest at twenty-one, and radiated class and good taste. She'd lived in India, Singapore, and Germany and currently lived in London where she'd been modeling at the Mattli design house and wore the clothes she'd acquired there.

Jessie, sixteen, from London, was surrounded by family members, her mother, brother, and a tiny sister who was wearing a dress with far too many layers of frilly underskirts, all come to see her off. Her mother, an outgoing, good-natured lady who, however, hadn't fully mastered her make-up and hair-bleaching techniques, was in charge, and I thought Jessie might possibly be happy that she was about to get some independence.

Annie, eighteen, was from Sheffield, with a broad Yorkshire accent to prove it. She was not glamorous but had the potential to be, with help, very attractive.

And then there was me.

As already mentioned, Peter Baker had told me to "look pretty" and, with this in mind, the previous evening I'd plucked my eyebrows and varnished my nails. Determined to spare no effort on this first day of my new life, I wore my newest dress. It displayed my figure nicely, with a straight skirt and belted waist and, a feature I loved, a wide-necked sailor-style white collar. Maybe not the most practical outfit for international travel, but Peter Baker had impressed on me that I had to look like a Bluebell, and I was certainly going to do my best. Other than my hair, which I'd put in a French pleat in an attempt to hold the tiny waves in place, I thought I gave an overall impression of being Bluebell material, if not the final product.

One of the experienced Bluebells had been given all of our tickets and the money for our travel expenses to hold. We'd be taking the boat-train to Newhaven, ferry to Dieppe, and train to Paris where we would be met by Miss Bluebell. Just as we were leaving Victoria Station, Peter Baker arrived, and after making sure that we were settled-in on the boat-train, turned to me and said, "At least they'll do something about your hair."

It took a whole day to travel from London to Paris, allowing time for conversation, time for savoring my first-ever day of foreign travel, and time for the realization that the moment was near when I would be faced with dancing alongside professional dancers. This certainly wiped away some of the pleasure of the day, but all I could do was tell myself, "Surely Miss Bluebell wouldn't have hired me if I couldn't make it?" And anyway, at that particular moment, on a ferry in the middle of the English Channel, it was useless worrying about it.

I had another concern; I wanted to fit in and be liked. I was going to have a miserable nine months if I didn't have any friends. Before we left Victoria I had already picked-up that all the "old" girls, including those we'd meet in Paris, had recently made contact with each other, and had selected who they were going to room with in the hotels and *pensiones*. Realizing I would be assigned a roommate, probably not one of my choosing if I didn't select my own, I quickly befriended Annie, the girl from Yorkshire. She agreed to be my roommate, and I believe it was a decision neither of us regretted. We were never best friends, but she was dependable and good-humored. I liked her.

On the train to Paris, my first view of a foreign country, I was surprised at the destruction France still showed, as the war had been over for fifteen years. At Paris Saint Lazare, we were met by Patrick, Miss Bluebell's twenty-year-old son, and Vera, the Captain of our troupe. It was evening by then and Miss Bluebell had arranged for taxis to take us past the illuminated sights of the city, including the Champs-Élysée, Arc de Triumph, and the Eiffel Tower, ending up at Gare de Lyon, where we were met by Miss Bluebell, her fifteen-year-old daughter, a mongrel dog, and the remaining four Bluebells.

There were Christine and Kate, twenty-two and twenty-three, both very experienced Bluebells. Upon being introduced, Christine asked me what my dancing experience was. Her response: "Oh, you're one of those!" Next there was Sophie, from The Hague, aged sixteen, who, I'd already been told was the "most beautiful Bluebell." They hadn't been exaggerating. She was beautiful. Thick, dark hair, blue/green eyes and a radiant smile. Her heritage was Indian, French, and Portuguese and, at sixteen, already an utterly charming young woman. My reaction: "Wow, fancy waking up every morning, looking in the mirror, and seeing that face." And if that wasn't enough, she spoke English well enough to be extremely funny. Overall, she was utterly captivating!

Monica, seventeen, from Brussels, was the other new girl. Tall, even for a Bluebell, and quiet, because she spoke no English. However, with translation from Sophie (Flemish and Dutch being similar languages), I learned she had as little dance experience as me. I was relieved and very happy to see her!

And then there was Vera, the Captain. She was an attractive woman of twenty-nine, who exuded self-confidence. She'd been the Captain of the first Bluebell troupe to appear in Las Vegas in the mid-1950s, and worked at the Lido, and in Buenos Aires and countless other cities around the world. Her French was good enough for our travel requirements and she appeared to know exactly what had to be done to get us where we had to be. I had full confidence in her.

We were put back into taxis and taken to dinner, where I saw and ate my first steak. (Prior to that evening I thought beef only came stewed or roasted.) We were late arriving back at the station but, just in time for departure, all twelve of us were safely boarded. Once on the Milan train, as I changed into slacks ready for the night's journey, I took the time to look back on my day—leaving my room in Chelsea, crossing the English Channel, traveling through the French countryside, and finally seeing the sights of Paris. Everyone was friendly, and the new girls, including me, were treated as though we belonged. I momentarily forgot about my balletic shortcomings and settled down to enjoy my new circumstances.

The night's journey turned out to be a long, miserable, and uncomfortable crush. We were twelve girls sleeping in two compartments, lying on six couchettes (benches folding out from the walls) in each of the two compartments, each girl with an overnight suitcase. The logistics of getting us all settled were tough, and throughout the night we were disturbed, first at a passport checkpoint at the Swiss border and later at the Italian border, and throughout the night by "inspectors," miscellaneous uniformed men, hoping to get a glimpse of a bare leg.

Vera had told us that "word would be out" that the Bluebells were arriving in Milan, so, in our cramped quarters, we all got "dolled up" for our 8:15 a.m. arrival at the train station, where the press would be waiting for us. We were to be disappointed; no press were waiting, so off we headed to our new home, our *pensione*, leaving our large suitcases to be delivered later in the day.

The *pensione* was located five minutes from the Duomo, Milan's glorious Gothic cathedral, just across the Piazza and around a corner. We entered the *pensione* by first stepping through a small pedestrian door cut into large carriage doors, which opened to the cobbled courtyard of a four storied building which, from the hours of business and the sound of typewriters through the open windows, appeared to be mainly offices.

One of the doors was the entrance to our *pensione*, and upon our arrival we were shown to our rooms and served with a continental breakfast (coffee and rolls, and a dab of butter and jam); then we walked a few blocks to the theater, the Teatro Lirico, our second home for the next two and a half months.

The Lirico had quite a history. It was built in 1779 as the opera house to serve Milan's non-aristocracy while, a few blocks away, La Scala was being built for the aristocracy. It had been originally built in the horseshoe style, with rows of boxes around the horseshoe-shaped walls but, following a fire in 1938, had been rebuilt in the modern style, with orchestra seating and a balcony above.

Upon our arrival we were met by Lee Sherman, the show's choreographer. I'd met him at the audition in London the week before and, after giving me a second look, he asked, "Do I know you?" I felt so insecure I was thrilled for this little recognition. We were then introduced to "the boys"—six male dancers, five Italians and one Spaniard, who were already rehearsing.

After being measured for our costumes, we were given the rest of the morning off to rest and told to return to the theater at 3 p.m. for our first rehearsal.

Things I'd learned so far: all the girls were immensely proud to be Bluebell Girls, me included; in the past, girls who couldn't learn the choreography had been sent home.

At 3 p.m. we were back at the theater, and at 3:30 p.m. Miss Bluebell arrived, having flown from Paris. The press also (finally) arrived and the twelve of us were photographed with Miss Bluebell, still wearing the dresses we'd traveled in, on stage, in the street, and finally, on the roof of the theater, which was arrived at by means of a narrow, somewhat rickety, staircase in the highest reaches of the theater; a challenge in a straight skirt and high heels.

During the photo session, our large suitcases had been delivered to the *pensione*, so those of us who hadn't carried our rehearsal gear in our overnight bags, that is, the new girls, rushed back to the *pensione* to pick up tights, leotards and shoes. We arrived back at the theater in time to hear Miss Bluebell's pep talk about working hard, and that she was proud of us, and then she was gone, back on her way to Paris, and we were back on stage for a forty-five-minute rehearsal. (The photo taken on the street appeared in the next day's Milan newspaper, and the one taken on the roof, in a national magazine several weeks later.) I had difficulty learning one of the steps, but after practicing later in the day, seemed to get it. I was told we would be starting serious work the next day and that it was going to be very hard work.

We ate dinner at the *pensione*, where all of us sat at one table, with Vera, our Captain, at the head. In the show, Vera was simply one of the dancers, but everywhere else, if you could name it, she did it: she was our mother, our father, as well as our boss. Her immediate responsibility was making the five new girls look, dance, and behave like Bluebells. The group dinners gave her the opportunity to lecture us on the many things we needed to be lectured on. Our first evening's lesson: whenever we appeared in public we had to "look good"—with "public" taking on a very broad definition that included the theater, shops, restaurants, and even the reception desk at the *pensione*. "Looking good," Vera made clear, meant that lipstick and eye liner, but no eye shadow and no foundation (unless your skin wasn't clear) were to be worn at all times, and hair had to be done in an approved style. The popular hairstyles were the page-boy, the flip, the beehive, and the French pleat; Vera decided which one suited you best, taking into consideration the length of your hair.

Rehearsals started at 10 a.m the next day, but before that I had one glorious night's sleep, not having seen a bed since I left London, seemingly days ago. On my way to the theater that morning I bought a pair of sneakers because, so I was told, they were a necessity as they were more comfortable than thin-soled ballet shoes, and they wore far better. Rehearsals then started in earnest, with us learning the steps to two dances: a cha-cha-cha, where, before the choreography was finalized, we danced many pirouettes, ending each segment with a cha-cha-cha; and a number with graceful hand and head movements, inspired by the classic East Indian dances. Sylvia, one of the new girls, had lived in India and had learned the original dance, so was welcomed by the choreographer, working with him to ensure that our hand, arm, and head movements were as close to authentic as possible. This didn't win her any points with Vera, who wasn't happy to see a new girl rising to the position of assistant to the choreographer, even if it was for only one number.

On that first day we rehearsed six hours, and I discovered early in the day that learning each sequence of steps was difficult. It was a skill I didn't possess. To add to my stress, I was desperately trying to fit in with the group of twelve girls, with whom the only thing I felt I had in common was my height. I was thankful that I hadn't been sent to Las Vegas, where I surely would have been even more out of my depth. I was also thankful that the group included Monica who, like me, had never previously done any "modern" style dance. Surely, I reasoned, they wouldn't send two of us home! It was a pity we didn't speak the same language and couldn't fully commiserate—instead we exchanged very slight sympathetic smiles, not daring to smile too broadly when we were so obviously in a show where we had such little right to be.

At dinner that evening Vera made a point of criticizing Jessie, Annie, and Monica, whose transgressions included slouching at the dinner table and wearing a pale shade of lipstick rather than a true red. Annie's unkempt eyebrows did not escape scrutiny, and she spent ninety minutes after dinner in Vera's room having them neatened. Stray hairs were eliminated and the remaining hairs were shaped to enhance her eyes. Every evening that week one of the new girls was summoned to Vera's room to further their transformation into a full-fledged Bluebell.

Vera was kind about my appearance, even announcing at dinner one evening that I had an "identical mouth, smile

29

and nose" to Grace Kelly. My shortcoming, she felt—and I agreed— was my hair. Wavy, frizzy, and a nondescript shade of brown, my hair had always been unmanageable; I was thrilled at the promise of finally having a good-looking head of hair. Vera created an elaborate (by today's standards) up-swept hairdo that stood high on my head, and which required me to see her early each morning so she could fix it before I left for the theater. She told me that my hair would become straighter when it was pulled tight and lacquered every night in the show, but as that might not be sufficient, I should also wear hard—and very uncomfortable—rollers to bed each night, which I did, though I wasn't happy about it. I want-ed to look like a Bluebell, and Bluebells didn't have heads of curly, kinky hair. Now and then I wouldn't use the rollers and I would lie in bed fearful that Vera would walk in and find I'd disobeyed her. And one more thing: she suggested that I regularly go to the hairdressers for a shampoo and set and "get a rinse, dark or red." When she came up with this sug-gestion, I made no response. As there was no way I was going "dark or red," I reckoned to "best let the moment pass."

The first week raced by and we rarely had a moment to ourselves. Although I didn't enjoy the time it took to "look good at all times," that effort was nothing compared to the level of anxiety learning the dance routines was giving me. I quickly realized that the hours I'd spent in ballet class in Lon-don had not prepared me for this job. Yes, it had prepared me for some aspects: I understood the dance terminology used by the choreographer and, once I'd learned a sequence of steps, my body movement bore a resemblance to the more experienced dancers, but it hadn't prepared me to memorize those dozens of dance steps to begin with.

By the third day, as soon as the more experienced girls had picked up the subtle and complicated hand movements of the Indian number, now referred to as the "*Orientale*," the choreographer added the accompanying foot movements—and then head and neck movements. Though the movements weren't physically difficult, memorizing the timing of each stamp of the bare foot (our costume included bells attached to our stamping feet), the direction of the leg, and the angle of the raised ankle, was too much. I was struggling.

Even those new girls who'd had years of dance training were having a hard time, so I could only assume that learning sequences of dance steps, at the speed necessary when rehearsing a new show, was not part of any amateur dancer's training. It's a skill that has to be picked up on the job.

Meanwhile, Annie's physical transformation continued. She was the only new girl who was required to change the color of her hair, and under Vera's direction, she spent an evening at the hairdressers and returned as a blonde. She looked simply lovely, an unbelievable difference. She was not only blonde but had been given a large beehive hairstyle which transformed her. She looked so sophisticated. Imagine my relief later that evening when I found out that her Yorkshire bluntness had survived the metamorphosis: we were discussing what time we should set the alarm for the following morning, and she quickly assured me she wouldn't be needing additional time to work on the new hairdo, because she wasn't "going to wear that fancy style tomorrow." And indeed, she didn't! And her more immediate concern: "How the heck am I going to sleep on this hair tonight?"

I really liked Annie. She was easy going, practical, funny, and even put up with me correcting her atrocious grammar. When I'd selected her as a roommate, I'd done well.

By the end of the first week, I still hadn't gone to the hairdressers and Vera wasn't happy. I pointed out that having a "shampoo and set" in the middle of rehearsals seemed pointless—weren't we racing around a stage, sweating, for hours each day? I would have to "get into the habit of looking good," she responded, adding that as the stars of the show would be arriving the following Monday, we all had to look particularly good.

It was around this time that Vera gave us another dictum: we were not to allow anyone to take our photographs without asking the identity of the photographer. If the photographer was from a magazine, we were instructed to ask for a business card and tell him he would have to apply to our Captain. She didn't elaborate on how we were to do this with our minimal Italian.

And then there was the matter of my body, and how it was coping with the non-stop punishment it was receiving. I'd not had an active life. Only ten days prior, I'd been sitting in an office taking shorthand dictation—my evening ballet classes certainly hadn't prepared me for this. By the end of the first day, the backs of my legs ached, and by the end of the first week the soles of my feet were sore. My lower legs swelled so much that my ankle bones were no longer visible, and they didn't reappear until the end of rehearsals.

The physical problems were nothing, just a passing inconvenience. Far more significant was the obvious struggle four of us new girls, not just Monica and me, were having, and the very real possibility that we weren't going to make it as Bluebell Girls.

At the beginning of the second week of rehearsals, Carlo Dapporto, the star of the show, arrived at the theater like Italian royalty, accompanied by a retinue of smartly dressed, portly, Italians. Also with him were other members of the show's cast and a photographer from *Oggi* magazine, there to record the event. Much kissing and hugging went on amongst the new arrivals and later we girls were photographed many times, both with and without Dapporto.

Then it was back to work, but first some background on Dapporto: he was a comedian and actor who had toured Italy in shows similar to ours, (the *Dapporto Spettacolo*) since the early 1940s, an original show each year. He was much loved by the audiences, particularly because he had continued his tours throughout the war, in spite of the obvious danger. Through the months, as I saw him interact with the audience, it appeared to me that he held a similar place in the hearts of Italians as Bob Hope held in the hearts of the English and was as big a star.

I'll also take this opportunity to describe the show's structure, keeping in mind it took me many weeks to figure this out. It was different from any show I'd seen produced in England. It had features of both a musical comedy and a variety show. It had a very weak story (so I was told; my Italian was never good enough to confirm this), that acted as a thread holding the scenes together in some kind of order and concluded with a satisfying finale in which the boy gets the girl. And, it was also somewhat like a variety show, in that it was a device for displaying the talents of its stars, Dapporto, Marisa del Frate, and the Bluebell Girls. The cast also included the male dancers, a vocal quartet, and six actors (five who were old friends of Dapporto who toured with the show every year, plus a sixth, Marisa's husband). I assumed they were there to develop the story. From listening to the applause, the audience came mostly to see the stars.

Rehearsals continued. We now worked from 10 a.m.- 1 p.m., 3-6 p.m., and 8-10 p.m., seven days a week, with an occasional evening off when the boys were rehearsing a number in which we weren't on stage with them.

By this time, we'd learned the basics of the Bluebell Presentation number, the first appearance of the Bluebell Girls in the show. The number began with the stage in darkness and a spotlight illuminating one girl's head and shoulders, while leaning through a royal-blue tinsel curtain that hung across the back of the stage. She was answering a traditional-style telephone, and saying something in Italian. This was repeated by several girls, and as they were standing at different levels on a very large staircase hidden behind the curtain, their upper-bodies popped out from random spots in the curtain.

Then the music for the number began. The curtain (and telephones) rose into the flies to reveal the Bluebells posed, with hands on hips, each girl on a different level of the staircase, facing away from the audience. We were wearing a strapless leotard of black sequined lace on a white background; with black satin trim around the legs, white fur trim around the top and diamanté decoration on both the leotard and in our hair. The stage lighting was adjusted to enhance our pose, and this was the moment, at 99% of performances, when the Bluebells received their first applause. Very gratifying, as we hadn't actually done anything yet!

We continued to face the back of the stage while twelve decorative wrought iron ovals, representing large dressing-table mirrors, descended from the flies, each coming to a halt when level with its assigned girl. Hanging on hooks at the sides of each mirror were a pair of long black satin gloves, a black sequin-covered wrap-dress and a very large white fur muff. To musical accompaniment, we completed the task of dressing, first the dress, then the gloves and finally the muff. Fully-dressed, looking like only Bluebells could look—gorgeous—we walked down the stairs, gracefully stepped along the *passerella*, gently waving the arm that was carrying the muff, where we'd receive more applause, and finally take our places on the stage, ready to begin our dance.

But I'm getting ahead of myself. I've just described the number as it would look on Opening Night. At this point in rehearsals, we were still learning the dance that came at the end of the dressing sequence.

One evening, Lee picked to pieces our performance of this number, and as I couldn't get a particular step, my performance was one that he particularly picked on. My eyes were brimming with tears, standing there knowing I was close to being thrown out of the troupe. The atmosphere was tense, but the moment passed, then things got worse. Lee and Rita Charisse, his assistant (and, incidentally, Cyd Charisse' ex-sister-in-law), started snapping at each other. I was learning that rehearsals are stressful for everyone, not just an under-prepared dancer!

Later, in the dressing room, Vera "let off," warning that some of us would find ourselves back in England if we didn't improve. Meanwhile, Lee constantly alluded to four of us being "not up to the standard of the others." While I knew the unfortunate little group definitely included me, Monica, and Jessie, the fourth person had to have been one of the other two new girls, Annie or Sylvia. Sylvia had previously only had ballet training, with no modern dance experience, and that resulted in some problems, but she shone in the *Orientale*. Or it might've been Annie, who didn't move gracefully and had a hard time exuding "sexy." The company had already nicknamed her "Sportiva."

There were also moments of humor, some unwittingly caused by Lee, who for long hours each day, endeavored to communicate with twenty members of the company—eighteen dancers plus a pianist and a drummer—only eleven of whom spoke or understood English, the only language he spoke. Kate's Italian was fluent, though, and Vera spoke Spanish, which helped a bit, and Rita, the boys and the musicians spoke some French (as a second language), so rehearsals were continually interrupted to allow for multiple chains of translation. If Rita was around, she would pass on Lee's instruction in French, and Monica, who only understood Flemish, received all of her direction via Sophie, in Dutch. The situation was an ongoing annoyance to Lee, his level of irritation rising when he was pointing out errors of any sort, and in particular with Mario, the pianist, when he started playing at the wrong place in the music. One day, in desperation, Lee shouted, "Oh, for God's sake, someone tell that man in French that he goofed!" I lived for these moments, because they meant I was out of the spotlight.

The day after Dapporto arrived was Vera's thirtieth birthday. On the previous night, after our evening meal, we had all squeezed into her room to wish her "Happy Birthday" and to give her a gift, a silk scarf. To us, Vera had reached an age when she should be checking out graveyards. The next day, her birthday proper, she treated us all to *panettone* and *spumoni*, yet another first for me. And, being the Bluebell Captain, she received flowers from Dapporto.

Once we'd learned the steps to our two big numbers, the Presentation and the *Orientale*, and also some lesser numbers, Lee introduced (for me it was an introduction) spacing and straight lines, two completely new concepts for me to master. I now had to worry about maintaining a consistent distance from my neighbors in front of me and on the sides, all while dancing. Though I was often positioned on the back row at the end, near the stage wings, without many neighbors, during a dance I moved around the stage, so I always had to be aware of where I was, and the distance between me and other dancers. Therefore, there was no spot on stage where spacing didn't matter.

If I felt sorry for myself, which I did, Monica was having a far worse time. On numerous occasions she told Sophie, who passed it on to the rest of us, that she wanted to throw herself under a tram: she didn't want to be in Milan, but also didn't want to go home. I so wished that I could talk to her. We could have commiserated with each other, even though I could see that we had different methods of handling our shame; while

Monica always looked incredibly unhappy, I was the reverse, always attempting to appear upbeat and confident. That was my strategy for handling the stress and it stopped me from crying!

There was one way in which I was in a better place than most of the girls. Many of them had boyfriends, all in other countries, and were forever checking out the stage-door area of the theater, where we received mail, only to be repeatedly disappointed. I was more fortunate. Ian, my summer-boyfriend, now returned to Canada, wrote me long letters on a regular basis. (I was still planning on visiting him at the end of the contract; a plan which I kept to myself.) Though his dedication didn't help me learn the dance steps, the fact that somewhere on this planet someone thought I was special enough to write long letters to, helped me get through even the most miserable rehearsal days. The three best things in my life were food, sleep, and an unopened letter.

Around then we were introduced to the show's music. We'd first heard it on the day that Dapporto arrived, when the composer sat on the side of the stage with the star, singing the songs, accompanying himself on the guitar. Now, a week or two into rehearsals, the pianist incorporated the music into our rehearsals. Previously we'd been dancing to music that had the right number of counts but generic melodies.

From then on, the composer was at the theater regularly, receiving his instructions to increase or reduce the bars of music as the choreographer required. I was so impressed. The composer, Franco Pisano, had a career in movies, and I assume that expanding and reducing a musical theme is what movie composers do, but this was the first time I'd seen the skill up close. All the melodies in the show reflected popular Italian music of the era, and were immensely hummable, and once the show opened, all my working hours were accompanied by the sound of music that I loved to listen to.

At this time, we were shown the sketches of our costumes, drawn on gray paper with colored pencil. We could see they were going to make us look glamorous but as they were drawn on exaggerated elongated mannequins, we couldn't truly picture what we or the finished costumes were going to look like.

When, eventually, I went to the hairdresser for the first time, Vera instructed me to get the "Grace Kelly" style and added "very severe." By this she meant that my hair should be pulled off my face and some kind of pleat concocted at the back of my head. I did as I was told and I thought the result looked a little untidy and commented to Annie, "Grace Kelly never looked like this," but Vera liked it, so it was money well spent.

Late during the second week, we went through the complete Presentation number. Rita, in her critique, said that Monica was a thousand times better, but that the girl dancing next to me (probably Jessie) didn't know the steps. She didn't even mention me. I was out of the spotlight. It was a red-letter day.

By the third week of rehearsals all the dancers had swollen ankles, and even the experienced dancers' legs were bothering them. During breaks we headed for the seats in the stalls and put our legs up on the seat backs of the row in front. Lee and Rita were now regularly snapping at each other, and at one point, Rita was in tears. Someone said she'd had a breakdown and was going home to the States, which turned out to be merely a rumor, thankfully, as by then she had become my friend and mentor.

My life was still a bit of a see-saw: Vera would tell me one day that I was "coming along reasonably well," and I even received a compliment, in public, from Rita: "It's gratifying teaching Elizabeth because when she has it, she really has it."

Yet again though, a few days later, Lee was unhappy with the progress of the new girls. All twelve girls were grouped around him, with me, unfortunately, directly in front. He looked me straight in the eye and said, "four of the new girls' level of dancing is not up to the standard of the others." I fought back tears (that was the second time in two weeks, but happily the last) while thinking, "That's true, he's right." Unfortunately, because I happened to be standing in front, he was talking directly to me, which made everyone feel very sorry for me, so immediately following this uncomfortable episode, everyone was especially nice to me. First, Lee put his arm around me and patted my head, giving me hope that I wasn't going home, and afterwards, Vera took me aside and told me not to worry, she knew I was doing my best. By the next night, Lee assured me, "You're doing a lot better, baby," and I reckoned I was safe.

Rehearsal days followed a typical routine:

8 a.m.	Wake.
	Continental breakfast in our room. Get ready for the theater, which included fixing hair and face.
9:25 a.m.	Walk to the theater.
9:45 a.m.	Arrive at the theater.

10 a.m.-1 p.m.	Rehearsal, with two twenty-minute breaks.
1-3 p.m.	Lunch break. Go to a restaurant or eat fruit at the theater.
3-6 p.m.	Rehearsal, with two twenty-minute breaks.
6-8 p.m.	Tea break. Shower at the theater.
8-10 p.m.	Rehearsal.
10 p.m.	Take a second shower, walk back to the *pensione.*
11:15 p.m.	Supper at the *pensione,* do hand laundry
12:15 p.m.	Lights out.

To replenish our hard-working bodies, we found it necessary to continually feed ourselves and luckily there were convenient places to purchase food. Right next door to the theater was a trattoria, and backstage there was a bar where we could purchase, on credit if need-be, drinks both of the alcoholic and non-alcoholic variety, and food, such as toasted cheese-and-ham sandwiches and cake.

CHAPTER THREE

THE SHOW TAKES SHAPE

Late in the third week I was a beginner no longer, finding it a little easier to pick-up new dances. Things really were improving. We rehearsed the Presentation number and the only criticism I received was that the "sexy walk" I was meant to use while descending the large staircase, wasn't up to par. I reckoned I could learn that. First, I needed to look more closely to see how the other girls did it, and then imitate them; and, anyway, I was certain that once I was in stage make-up, hairdo, and costume, "sexy" would come more easily.

Our costumes were delivered, labeled plainly inside with the first name of a dancer. We were fitted for each of the ten costumes, and they were taken away again for final alterations.

Large pieces of the scenery began arriving on stage. It was important for the dancers, actors, choreographer, and stage director to know which bits of the stage couldn't be used by humans! Much negotiation went on between Lee and the stage designer, Giorgio. And it often seemed to us girls that Lee considered it easier for Giorgio to have scenery reconstructed than for Lee to change the choreography! It became a standing joke amongst us. If a number wasn't going right, we always suggested, "Let's get Giorgio to change the scenery."

43

And then there was the story: I'm sure that the Italians in the cast learned the story of the show. I never did, but here's my best stab: the hero, a Polish prince, played by Dapporto, lives in London, and is so royal that he has exclusive use of twelve call-girls. (The Bluebell's Presentation number is the audience's introduction to the call girls.) The Prince then walks in Hyde Park (surrounded by Bluebell Girls, looking ethereal rather than sexy) and has a dream, hence the *Orientale* number. He discovers that the woman in the dream is a Captain in the Salvation Army, so he joins the Salvation Army. Some women, who may or may not be the call girls (I never found out), also join the Salvation Army, which allows for a scene where we girls perform a marching number, while the vocal quartet sing and play brass band instruments. A bit later, in the Docks of London, the girls discover that the Prince, in Salvation Army uniform, isn't who he says, and the girls are angry and whip off capes and bonnets and reveal our Act I Finale costumes, whereupon, of course, we dance.

I never had any idea what the story of the second half of the show was. The Bluebell Girls opened the Act with a shower scene, and that was followed with a raucous pantomime scene in Victoria Station, and then a scene in a photographic studio, where we were models and, to close the show, the Finale takes place in Little Poland, an area of London, where Dapporto and Marisa finally come together in a celebratory event.

A week or so earlier, a photographer had come to the theater to take portraits of each of the girls to be displayed in the front of the theater and in the show's printed program. Vera gave me a high chignon with three strings of pearls wrapped around it, and applied bold eye-lines which added some glamour. I'd never felt so grand. The first photos were awful, so they hired one of Italy's top photographers, Elio Luxardo, to redo them. This time the photos were beautiful and company management would be using them to advertise the show. We girls immediately ordered copies to send home to our families.

The hair extensions Vera had ordered for each of the new girls had arrived by then. We paid 8,000 lire (£)—two days salary—for our "switches," which we wore whenever our look required an upswept hairstyle with a bundle of hair on the top. The extension was attached with hairpins to a high ponytail, then wound around several times to form a pile of hair on the top of the head, held in place with a hairnet, and then secured to the surrounding hair with yet more hairpins. This hairstyle became a great friend throughout the tour, on-stage and off: easy to manage with practice, and always smart and attractive looking. Anytime anyone's hair wasn't fit for public display, she could attach what we called a "chignon," apply a little hairspray (or beer) to the wispy dangling bits of stray hair, and she'd immediately look not only glamorous, but several inches taller. *Voilà!* A Bluebell.

Financially-speaking, we were all comfortable. During rehearsals we were paid £4,000 per day, however, we were given only £2,000 daily and the remaining £14,000 was distributed at the weekend when the *pensione* bill of £11,000 a week plus extras, such as baths (yes, a bath was an extra! No wonder we took showers at the theater) came due. The Bluebell organization was smart to enforce our savings, as many of us were forever spending beyond our means and wouldn't have put money aside to pay the weekly bill. Once the show opened, we would receive £6000 per day, four times my pre-Bluebell earnings. Most of the girls saved nothing, though, because we ate at least one meal a day in a restaurant and spent a lot on our appearance, including many trips to the hairdressers for a daily "comb and lacquer," and a weekly "shampoo and set."

Starting the day I arrived in Milan I'd been saving money, so when three girls ran out of money before the end of the week, they borrowed from me, paying me back on payday. I quickly became the troupe's money-lender and was given the nickname "Bank of England," a position I held for many months into the tour. I have to admit that, during rehearsals, with my position in the troupe as precarious as it was, I was comforted to have a few of the girls beholden to me.

We were recognized everywhere we went in Milan which, with our non-existent social lives, was mainly in restaurants. As a group of tall, good-looking girls, we were gazed upon and admired whenever we were in public. After having been a frizzy-haired shorthand typist in London, ignored by all, needless to say, I found this a delightful experience.

With this attention came perks. One afternoon a group of us were having lunch when we met an English family, residents of Milan, who were sitting at a nearby table. The father came over to chat and asked me how I liked Italy. I told him, among other things, I missed Yorkshire pudding. He went off to talk to the chef and said he'd arranged for us to be served Yorkshire pudding. Indeed, when we returned to the restaurant the next day, we were presented with "Yorkshire pudding," which, in truth, resembled more of an omelette, but it made us feel very special.

We were still having dinner together at the *pensione* at the end of every workday. The old Bluebells hated spending their precious time off with Vera; they wanted to be independent, and the only independence available during rehearsals was to select your own restaurant for the late night meal. The new girls didn't have the same need to get away from Vera. For one thing, we'd never tasted independence in a foreign city, and, by this time, we were used to being critiqued over dinner. Eating together gave us the opportunity to get to know each other and to hear war-stories shared by the more experienced Bluebells.

One of our favorites was the story about the night at the Lido, when the stage elevators and the lights simultaneously malfunctioned. Girls who were standing offstage, chatting, were suddenly illuminated, in full view of the audience. Vera, waiting to go on stage, rushed to the electrician standing at his console, shouted above the music to tell him about the malfunction. The music was so loud she couldn't attract his attention, so she leaned across the hatch the showgirls used to get into the pool (yes, the Lido has a pool) to tap him on the shoulder, only to lose her footing and disappear into the water.

Vera could also be quite mean at the group dinners. One evening, she not only reprimanded Jessie for her bad table manners, but went on to tell her that she ate like a pig and was disgusting the girls who sat next to her so that it was turning them off their meal. No one spoke up in her defense. I remember thinking, "She's right, Jessie *does* eat like a pig."

The old Bluebells wanted to move to a hotel: the food at the *pensione* wasn't good, there was no running water in our rooms and the rooms weren't very clean, they complained. They also wanted to be away from Vera's watchful eye. Some of the newer girls, including me, wanted to stay in the *pensione*, which was less expensive than a hotel. If we left, we'd also be eating our late night meal in a restaurant every night, which would rack up the expenses. There were many discussions, and early on it had been six to six, but a vote sealed it eleven to one, with me the lone "stay" vote.

The *pensione* management wasn't happy about our exodus and Vera was having a hard time handling the situation, so "Mr. Libo" (whose real name was Marcel Leibovici), the Bluebell organization's business manager and Miss Bluebell's husband, was summoned to smooth things over.

Here's some background on Mr. Libo that I didn't know at the time: in the 1930s he was the Music Director at the Folies Bergère, in Paris, where Miss Bluebell's dancers, *Les Bluebell*, performed. By the time WWII broke out they had married and were parents to a baby son, Patrick. During the war, Mr. Libo, having Jewish grandparents, was interned. He escaped and made his way back to Paris where, for two and a half years, Miss Bluebell hid and supported him.

Before Mr. Libo arrived, I had decided I didn't like him, as it was common knowledge that he had bedded nearly a hundred Bluebells and, to make matters worse, he bragged about it. Putting that small matter aside, of his various functions within the Bluebell organization, the one that would affect us the most, was his intermittent check-ins on Bluebell Girls' performances around the world, as it was his job to ensure that our dancing remained up to the required standard. He prided himself on the fact that each visit he made to a troupe "in the field" was unannounced and unexpected. The result was that every girl knew that as they danced any number, in any performance, Mr.Libo might be hiding in the flies or out in the audience. The stories of his past efforts to surprise the girls were pretty funny, like the time the Bluebells were dancing at the Moulin Rouge in Paris, and there he was, onstage, inside the windmill!

My expectation was that, on this visit, he'd immediately watch a rehearsal to see how the new girls were coming along; he'd talk to the choreographers, talk to Vera and decide whether any of us should be replaced. My greatest hope was that he wouldn't even notice I was there.

To my relief, his most pressing interest was not our dancing, and instead he immediately set to work re-housing us, calming the irate *pensione* owners and finding us a hotel closer to the theater with showers available to us. Later in the day he met with us, and I was surprised to find that, in spite of having the unfortunate physical appearance of a frog, he was quite a charming man. He had just traveled from Venice where Bluebells were appearing at the Casino, and he showed us a copy of *Weekend* magazine with Bluebells featured on the cover and in the center pages, as well as a theater program, and photos of the Venice troupe and also photos of a troupe working in Glasgow. All the girls were intrigued to hear and read accounts of how our fellow Bluebells were faring. It was like hearing about the goings-on in the lives of some close cousins.

Mr. Libo also, somehow, arranged for us to take a day off from rehearsals, which Vera used as an opportunity to tell the new girls off for not being glamorous enough. "Everyone had been complaining," she said, without specifying about what, and added that hers had to be, "the most beautiful Bluebell troupe." The consequence for me was that I had to spend my vacation day purchasing a new rehearsal outfit and going to the hairdressers.

Joining the world of the Bluebells was akin to attending a "finishing school," where a central focus was on appearance, with less emphasis on deportment and etiquette, although those facets of our behavior weren't ignored. The advice we were given even included our selection of clothing. Vera wanted us to purchase only classic clothing, by which she meant clothes that had been fashionable a few years prior and would still be fashionable a few years hence. It was the way to build up a wardrobe of good-looking clothes. To that end we all looked forward to visiting the Milanese dressmakers once the show had opened and we had more free time. In addition, Vera was always willing to come shopping with us, which I later took her up on. I felt that purchasing clothes was making an investment and wearing classic-style clothing made sense. By the end of the tour, although I didn't have a large wardrobe, I felt attractive in every item.

Mr. Libo didn't stay long; only days after his arrival he returned to Paris. I knew that he had criticized other girls to their faces, so I was waiting with trepidation for him to speak to me before he left. He never did. It hadn't escaped me that on the days he had watched rehearsals I had done just about everything right, so my name hadn't "rung out" much. Later Vera shared with me that he was very pleased with me.

CHAPTER FOUR

WE OPEN IN MILAN

By mid-September we were in our fourth week of rehearsals, with the opening set for September 25th. Previously, we had worked alone but now we began working on numbers where other members of the company were on stage with us, usually one of the stars or the vocal quartet. We still rehearsed alone in the daytime, and then with other members of the company in the evening. If the stage was needed by non-dancers during the day, the dancers were shunted off into the theater's foyer to rehearse. Our hours became longer, initially until about 10:30 p.m. We were warned by Lee that eventually we'd be continuing into the early hours, because "Dapporto believes that that gets results." Lee didn't like this practice, but "the Italians like it," he said, "and we're in Italy!"

We spent more time sitting around waiting to be called for a particular scene, usually in the stalls with our legs hooked over the backs of the seats of the row in front, still taking care of our abused legs. The rehearsals themselves had become somewhat boring, and I found myself looking at my watch to see if it was time for a break. I wished the show would open, complete a successful stint in Milan, and then start touring so I could see more of Italy. Despite the boredom, I was glad to be where I was, in a show, in Milan, and having made it as a Bluebell Girl!

With the reduced hours of dancing, my ankles returned to their normal size, but I then had to contend with dancing in high heels and so developed sore shins. The longer workdays with the attendant lack of sleep, coming at the end of four weeks of very hard work, took their toll. Some of the girls became utterly exhausted, collapsing in the middle of a dance. I was fine as long as I had sufficient food and sleep. Annie and I had tried to keep the cost of meals down to one restaurant meal a day, snacking on fruit the rest of the time, but that no longer worked. We needed more calories, and Vera insisted that we have two full meals a day, to which we acquiesced. Even so, I had lost one-and-a-half inches from my hips.

I learned from the "old" Bluebells that even though the show would be starting in a couple of weeks, that would not be the end of rehearsals. Formal rehearsals would end, but we'd still have informal rehearsals, and once the choreographers left the show, Vera would likely change some of the numbers, which would necessitate yet more rehearsals.

The whole company—dancers, singers, actors, musicians—was tired. Everyone was getting testy, and tantrums were thrown over situations that should have been laughable. One of the boys was miffed because he wasn't paired with Sophie in a dance where we danced in pairs. Unable to figure out how to get what he wanted, particularly as he didn't speak English, he threw a fit when he was paired with a dancer who was taller than him. The rest of us saw the whole scene as ludicrous and just rolled our eyes.

The living conditions at the new hotel we had moved to were wonderful. Annie and I had one of the best rooms, large and bright, with space between the two beds, and our room, like all the others, had a wash basin with hot and cold running water, so we no longer had to share a bathroom with ten other girls. And—good news—Vera was housed on a different floor and, as we now went to a restaurant at the end of our workday, Vera no longer presided over our evening meal. The first evening, Giorgio, the scenery designer, dined with us and bought us drinks and I drank my first Cognac.

I was happier. There were some good things about these final weeks of rehearsals. We were no longer learning the long, complicated dances, but instead patching up and fitting bits together. It was still challenging, of course. While learning our big blockbuster dances was behind us, we were still learning smaller routines, so I still had plenty of opportunity to mess up. In a couple of the dances, we were learning to move in formations which had to be repeated and repeated in order to get them right. I was often the source of mistakes and the resulting "do-overs." Eleven girls would turn their heads left, military style—think Radio City Rockettes—mine would start to turn right, I'd immediately see my error, and zip left. But my future didn't seem to be in jeopardy any longer. Plus, my relationship with Lee had changed. One morning, after trying unsuccessfully to teach me to do a sexy walk, he assured me that I could never be a streetwalker! This was the first occasion we had exchanged any humor, and it felt good. I was still expected to practice as much or more than the rest of the girls and one afternoon, while taking a tea break, Lee and Rita walked past me and told me, pleasantly but directly, to quit my break and work on the steps from the previous rehearsal session.

In off moments, when the piano wasn't in use, I'd sit and play, attempting to play the show's music, trying to decipher the shorthand manuscript that the show's pianist, Mario, read from. The composer would smile at my attempts and the drummer would provide back-up, but the girls hated it. They told me in no uncertain terms that they had to listen to those melodies when they were working, and they didn't want to hear them during their breaks. Apparently, they did not find me as impressive as I thought I was! Anyway, the piano had by then been moved from the stage to the orchestra pit, and was harder for me to get to, so there was no more piano playing for me. We were now hearing all the show's music played by a full orchestra. It was glorious. We'd heard all the melodies with only a piano and drummer for so long.

During the run of the show, I never tired of hearing the music. It was beautiful. I quickly realized that a bonus of dancing for a living, one I'd never given a thought to before, was that whenever I was working, I was listening to wonderful music. Even between our numbers, when we weren't on stage, there was other music being performed which we heard over the sound system in the dressing room.

Our photos were now appearing in magazines like *Marie Claire* and *Oggi*, and the posters for the show were on display around Milan. All of our individual names were listed. I was Bridget Dale, taken straight from my passport, Bridget being the first of my three given names. Dapporto was happy when he found that there was a Bridget amongst the Bluebells. Those were the days of Brigitte Bardot, Europe's number-one sex kitten, and maybe he hoped that a Bridget listed amongst the Bluebells would arouse some curiosity and increase the audience numbers—even though I was known to all as Elizabeth.

Now that I had the dancing more or less under my belt, Vera took on the matter of my appearance. One morning she had a go at me, accusing me of "letting the side down" by looking like the way I did. She told me that, not only should I have my hair shampooed and set once a week, which I'd begun a couple of weeks previously, but I should also go to the hairdresser each day to have my hair combed. She also told me I wasn't wearing enough makeup, my particular transgression being that I was not wearing eyeliner. I had nothing against eyeliner but hadn't experimented with it previously because I knew that if I initiated any change to my appearance, and Vera liked it, I'd be locked into including it in my make-up regime from that moment on. It was wiser to wait for Vera to see the need.

The next day I started wearing eyeliner and it greatly improved my appearance. Vera had been right.

Vera was right about lots of things, but I didn't like being dictated to, and a definite downside of the job was that my boss was within a few feet of me every waking hour. There was no "going home" in the evening and getting a little relief! On the bright side, the experienced Bluebells assured me that once the show opened, Vera wouldn't be as omnipresent, and wouldn't be able to keep track of my hairdresser visits.

In some of the numbers we danced on the *passerella*, a shaky catwalk that runs parallel to the stage between the orchestra pit and the first row of the audience, with a walkway leading to the stage at each end. A majority of the theaters we performed in had a *passerella*. We first danced along it during the Presentation number, after we came down the staircase and before we started the dance on stage. Then later, the dancers, along with the rest of the cast, would make our way across it at the end of Act I and Act II, representing curtain calls. First the male dancers went, then the Bluebells, followed by the actors, the vocal quartet and the stars. We learned combinations of steps to be performed as we moved across the *passerella*, three sets for the end of Act I, and three more at the end of Act II. Each combination was performed to a melody introduced during the foregoing Act. If the audience's applause was strong while the whole cast progressed across the *passerella* then the dancers would begin another round. If the applause continued with intensity, we might dance eight or nine "*passerellas*," repeating the three dances. If the audience was less enthusiastic, we would dance two or three.

Vera did her best to make sure we had enough sleep. As the workdays lengthened, and we were working until 1:30 a.m. and still expected to be at the theater at 10 a.m. the next morning, Vera insisted that, during the day, we be sent back to the hotel for a nap. And there were others getting less sleep than us. The carpenters told us that they were working both day and night, and it was not uncommon to see wardrobe and stagehands sleeping at the side of the stage.

On the day of the unofficial dress rehearsal, three days before the opening, we started a standard rehearsal at 10 a.m. and worked until 2 p.m. We then had a break until 8 p.m. but as Vera was doing my makeup, I had to be back at the theatre at 6:30 p.m., so after having a meal I went back to the hotel and had less than two of hours of sleep. We then worked until 3 a.m. Even so, we didn't get through the whole show, not getting to the Finale or several sketches that came before. However, even without rehearsing the Finale, the rehearsal was extremely important for the Bluebells because it was the first run-through wearing our costumes, when we found out what the timing would be for our costume changes.

What we found out was that we were on stage a lot, and that the show, which lasted four hours, went by incredibly quickly because we had so many costume changes. Our longest break between numbers was thirty minutes, and in those thirty minutes we had to get ready for the next number, which took fifteen minutes, and then lay out our costumes for the following number, the *Orientale*, when we would have only four minutes to make the change.

During those four minutes we first took off our costume from the Hyde Park scene; that is, gloves, a diaphanous ballet dress (*à la Les Sylphides*), shoes and tights, and a floral hair decoration and our chignon—plus the many hairpins holding it on. To speed up this operation, the dressers undid the fasteners down the back of the dresses and then whisked them away, hanging them where they could be found for the next show. We girls kept up the momentum, pulling on stretch pants, and wriggling into a bodice, the two main pieces of the *Orientale* costume. A dresser would be waiting, ready to fasten the hooks and eyes, and buckle the decorative narrow gold leather bridle that wrapped around our shoulders, and while they were busy at our backs, we girls attached a head-dress firmly enough that it would withstand a series of pirouettes, and then snapped on two sets of bracelets, one for the upper arm and one for the lower. We immediately ran to the stage, in bare feet, and once we arrived in the wings, we stuck additional hairpins into the headdress, and, finally, before the *Orientale* began, attached bells to our feet.

Every night there was near panic in the dressing room. Only a few moments later, though, the audience would see twelve beautifully dressed, beautifully groomed Bluebells on stage, each displaying the serene smile of an East Indian dancer. The contrast still makes me smile today.

The next day we received Lee's critique. He announced that the dressing scene that preceded the Presentation number—when we were standing on the staircase—was going to be completely revised, because the Bluebells hadn't succeeded at getting dressed as we had rehearsed, putting on each garment to a particular number of counts of the music. Instead, Lee wanted us to start the number dressed and take off the gloves, dress and muff and hang them on the dressing tables and then dance the number wearing only our leotards. Vera was apoplectic when she heard this pronouncement. She was adamant that the Bluebells wouldn't be dancing their opening number in anything but their full costume. We had more rehearsals and ended up with one modification to the routine: we would begin the scene already wearing one of the gloves, so we'd only have to put on the second one, which gave us a few additional seconds to complete our dressing sequence on time.

Mr. Libo, having arrived from Paris right before this dress rehearsal, also had his take on the show, which was that the script was awful, and the only good things in the show were the costumes; to be specific, those worn by the two leads, Dapporto and Marisa del Frate, and the Bluebells.

It turned out, once the show was open, the audience was more generous with its critique than Mr. Libo had been! A number they always thoroughly enjoyed was the shower scene, danced to a cha-cha-cha rhythm. Some of us wore short towels wrapped around our bodies, exposing shoulders and legs, while others wore a not particularly brief, two-piece swimsuit made from toweling. All our heads were covered with toweling turbans. While we cha-cha-cha'd around the stage, we were all involved in various activities. I remember Vera was deeply engrossed in a newspaper, and Kate, Deanna, and Sophie each had a chair they picked up and handled in some way, and all this went on while one of the cast members, an actress, sang a solo.

The audience particularly enjoyed the routine Sylvia and I carried out near the front of the stage. We first cha-cha-cha'd across the stage, from the left wings to the right wings, holding up and hidden behind, a very large towel, exposing only our heads above and feet and ankles below. We hid in the wings for a bit and then crossed again in the opposite direction. Then we crossed yet again, in the original direction, but while we crossed, we rolled into the towel, towards each other, our bottoms wiggling from side to side as we cha-cha-cha'd. Finally, we crossed the stage for the last time, again hidden behind the large towel but with Monica between us, keeping her head hidden below the towel, but exposing her ankles and feet, so the audience saw six feet and only two heads. They never failed to laugh.

The next night, at the dress rehearsal proper, we performed the *Finalissimo* for the first time with costumes, and it was revealed that what we'd rehearsed was impractical and had to be scrapped. The scene was set in Little Poland, an area of London, and the Bluebells were wearing stylized Polish national costumes made of heavy-weight white satin, edged in Persian lamb fur (faux, I assume). The dress was richly decorated with beaded embroidery in red and gold and the lower portion of the sleeves and headdress were made of white organza with gold lace edging; the sleeves, billowy, and the headdress, large and structured. The dress had an underskirt and was worn over a hooped crinoline. To top it off we wore gold, dangly earrings and a decorative gold necklace, and long red gloves, that had yet more gold embroidery. There was hardly an inch of us that was uncovered, and yet we were a sight to behold!

The girls were to be handed baskets of flowers by the boys, each flower having a foot-long stem with a round weight on the bottom, and we were to "plant" each flower on the stage. When a basket was emptied, a boy was to bring us another basket. It was planned that we would plant 1,200 flowers, partially covering the stage, leaving an aisle down the center through which the stars would walk to the front of the stage. The dress rehearsal was a cross between chaos and disaster. I dutifully planted my first basket of flowers and looked for "my" flower boy, who was supposed to bring me additional baskets of flowers. He was nowhere to be seen. Later he told me he had been crossing round the back of the stage, rather than across the front, where I was—why, I never found out.

Our costumes were the cause of much of the chaos. Every time we moved, with our wide, heavy skirts, we knocked down the flowers already planted, and once the planting was completed, we were to sit on the less-than-clean stage in those beautiful white dresses—yet another bad idea. To top it off, Annie had found herself surrounded by planted flowers and cut off from the area of the stage where she needed to be. Being our "sportiva," she decided that there was only one way out and picked up her skirt and crinoline and took one gigantic stride over the flowers. At first, we were all aghast—weren't we the beautiful, graceful Bluebells?—and then everyone broke into uncontrollable laughter. It was the final straw. From then on, for the remainder of the tour, there were just a few baskets of flowers either hanging from girls' arms or placed along the perimeter of the stage.

The next night was the press show, and more press than expected came, filling most of the orchestra section. There was a wonderful moment at the beginning of the Presentation. The lights were very dim, and the audience could only make out the girls' silhouettes on the staircase behind the fringe, and they broke out in applause. It made us feel fabulous. I knew then, for the first time, what it was to be a Bluebell. We were not merely twelve long-legged, well-dressed, beautifully groomed girls, standing on a stage in Italy; we were the beneficiaries of the hard work of all the Bluebells that had gone before us. What's more, by our beautiful appearance and elegant stance, we were perpetuating the Bluebell mystique. We couldn't have known, we couldn't have even guessed, that that mystique would prevail through many decades to come.

This was the first performance in which we wore our blonde wigs in the Sexy Studio number. We were supposed to be pin-up models in a photography studio and our costume called for a shoulder-length blonde wig that draped over one eye. At the following day's rehearsal, during which Lee gave us his notes on the previous evening's performance, we weren't surprised when he told us that we wouldn't be wearing the wigs again. We'd already heard from Vera that Mr. Libo thought they looked cheap. Lee had agreed, and they were gone.

Opening night itself appeared to be a moving target. There were posters around town with a date: September 25th. When we weren't going to be ready by that date, it was changed to the 26th and dozens of posters were reprinted and re-posted around the city. Maybe the audience consisted only of guests because I never did understand how this system worked if there was a paying audience.

The show did indeed open on Monday, September 26th. While we were getting made-up, several boxes of chocolates, bouquets of roses, and about seven telegrams arrived, the latter being from the other troupes, including those in Las Vegas, Glasgow, and the Lido. More mysteriously, we were each given a packet of toothpaste, with a single red rose attached. I still regret not having roses to present to Rita that night. She'd been very good to me during the previous weeks, and I should've shown my appreciation.

The show went quite well. Embarrassingly, I didn't get my dress done up in the Presentation number, so it flapped around while I danced; a very good reason for new girls to dance in the back row. At the end, when there were lots of "*passerellas*," one of the girls was counting, and lost count at nine. The audience, eager to demonstrate their enthusiasm, surged forward, picking off all the flowers that were decorating the edges of the *passerella* and side boxes, and tossed them at us. After the show, the whole company was taken out for a celebratory meal. The Bluebells arrived at the restaurant later than the rest of the company and as we walked up the center of the room everyone burst into applause. We got to bed around 4:30 a.m. It had been a good evening.

Although I'd made it to Opening Night, I still wasn't particularly self-confident. Ever aware that a number of the older Bluebells were still evaluating me, I felt a bit of a fraud, but this feeling was leaving me, bit by bit. I had proven that I could give the appearance, on stage, of being a Bluebell. That had to give me some legitimacy.

Privately, so private I would never whisper it to another girl, I felt relaxed and thrilled. Rehearsals had ended and I had made it!

The next day was Tuesday: payday. I bought a couple of pairs of shoes, one brown and one black. My old shoes would be demoted, now only to be worn when walking to the theater on rainy days.

CHAPTER FIVE

A DANCER'S LIFE

egular performances of the show began the next day, seven days a week, with two performances on Sundays, with the evening show running from 9:30 p.m. to 1:30 a.m.

We soon settled into a routine, and would be awakened at 1 p.m. with a continental breakfast served in bed. It was my task to greet the waiter who brought in the meal. One day, I happened to mention "the man who brings in breakfast" to Annie, who was a very deep sleeper, and she responded, "What man?" She never did set eyes on him during those remaining five weeks we were in Milan. For the rest of the afternoon, on days when we didn't have an afternoon show, we'd lie in bed chatting, often joined by other girls, or reading, writing letters or doing crosswords.

Other activities in which we indulged were shopping, viewing the sights (rarely), visiting the hairdresser, and when scheduled, attending rehearsals. Our afternoons ended with a meal in a *trattoria* right before going to the theater, and on Sundays, when we gave two performances, a local *trattoria* brought food into the dressing room between the shows. And finally, at the end of our workday we ate at one of two late-serving restaurants that were in walking distance of the theater and hotel. And then back to the hotel, to wind down, with lights off around 4 a.m.

Now that I had time to socialize, my eyes were suddenly opened to how widespread "rule-breaking" was within the Bluebells. Early on in rehearsals I'd been made aware of the very strictest Bluebell rule; one which, if broken, meant termination: ***Thou shalt not socialize with members of the company.***

I'd been told that we should be pleasant, but nothing more, when interacting with the men in the company. That was it. I understood the reasons for the rule, but it still felt odd that at one moment I was "being pleasant" to one of the boys while we stood on the side of the stage, and the next moment we were arm in arm, warm body against warm body, smiling into each other's face, galloping round the stage together. To further impress upon the new girls how seriously Miss Bluebell took this rule, we'd been told that three girls had been fired in the previous year's Dapporto Tour for breaking this rule, two of them for dating members of the vocal quartet who were with the show again this year.

During rehearsals all the girls, including me, were aware that Vera had been dating Giorgio, the scenic designer; it was the best known, and least kept secret around. But then I found out that lots of girls were dating men in the company. It was secret, but it was only a secret from Vera. We didn't have bedtime roll call, so only your roommate knew for sure. As it was well-known that I had a boyfriend in Canada, I was merely an observer, and anyone not on a date would come to our room to chat while we waited for girls to come home. I could see plenty of good reasons why Miss Bluebell would have this rule and I'm sure it was made as a result of her long experience directing troupes of mostly young, single (and attractive) dancers. But even though the rule was commonly broken, it still served its purpose in that the enforced secrecy ensured that no one was ever late for a show after returning from a surreptitious car trip, no couples chatted backstage leading to a missed entrance, and jealousies were never overt, because that would break the lovers' cover. However, this rule widened the gap between Vera and the girls because only Vera would report liaisons to Miss Bluebell. There was strong loyalty amongst the other eleven girls.

A few days into the run of the show Vera let me know that the chignon I wore on stage wasn't large enough. I would need to buy a second switch. The one she'd purchased on my behalf was made from very fine hair so it didn't create a big enough bun. I was told to buy one made of nylon—which was generally cheaper than real hair, thankfully—to wear under the one I already owned. This was a burdensome task because buying anything that I couldn't point to or wasn't a commonly used item found in a restaurant or backstage, the only places where I practiced my Italian vocabulary, wasn't easy. I visited several hairdressers and explained what I wanted, in a mixture of English (fluent), French (schoolgirl) and Italian (meagre). They would indicate that they didn't have what they thought I wanted, or they only had it in black, and direct me to other hairdressers who they thought might have what they thought I wanted. Eventually there was a meeting of minds, and a hairdresser produced a switch made from real hair close to my hair color, and, good news, it turned out to be less expensive than nylon hair. My chignon problems were solved, and Vera was happy.

Milan was the only stop on the tour where we routinely socialized with people outside of our show. *The Josephine Baker Show* was on at another theater in Milan and some of the performers would eat at the same restaurant as us, one of the few that served meals after 2 a.m. A few of the girls knew members of the *5 Brutos*, an Italian male vocal group, consisting of a soloist and four slapstick cohorts. They'd appeared in the same show in Stockholm. We also got to know several members from a band of slapstick comedians/musicians who we referred to as the Crazy Band. We'd chat over dinner, and some of the girls would then go off on dates with the men. From my perspective, even if I wasn't interested in dating, it was good to sit and chat with folks who both spoke fluent English and were not in the *Dapporto Spettacolo*. And they were so funny! I'd never had personal contact with comedians before. It had never crossed my mind that people who make a living making people laugh are also funny when they're off-stage. And it was nice to be reminded that there was life outside of the Lirico and the Hotel Candidezzo!

As it happened, the Crazy Band left Milan before us. *The Josephine Baker Show* wasn't paying its way and, so we were told, five dancers, the wardrobe mistress and one of the bands had been given one day's notice and the Crazy Band had been given five days' notice. Our friends in the Band told us that their contract stated that if they were at the theater each night, playing their instruments, they could get paid, so they planned on sitting in their dressing room playing a pile of records and then, of course, demand their wages. This didn't work out and hiring a lawyer also didn't help, and a few nights later they came to the restaurant to say goodbye; they were returning to England the following day.

Milan was, as it still is, known as a center of high fashion. Where better to begin putting together an elegant wardrobe? A few days after the show opened four of us went off to visit a dressmaker, strongly recommended by Vera and other Bluebells who'd previously worked in Milan.

Vera had advised me to order a winter dress and coordinating coat that would be the basis for my winter wardrobe. The dressmaker's suite was in a grand old building, and the first room we entered, the outer room, was sparsely furnished but elegant. There were a few occasional chairs, small tables, and a rack on which a few dresses hung. On the tables were thick, heavy, glossy women's Italian fashion magazines. I selected a short-sleeved, knee length, straight dress from the rack, and then scoured the magazines to find a coat that would go over it. I wasn't overly enthusiastic about the coat I chose, since I was somewhat limited in the style I could select because it had to go over the woolen dress. Anyway, it appeared elegant in the magazine photograph, had three-quarter sleeves which I liked, and I preferred it to anything else I saw.

Next, I had to select the fabric. Swatches of woolen fabric were attached to thick pieces of board and I immediately sorted through the boards to find a fabric that had both dress-weight and coat-weight fabric in the identical color and a similar weave. There was only one fabric duo that met the criteria, and it was dark peacock blue, so I didn't have any choice over the matter; my dress and coat were dark peacock blue.

All four of us ordered clothing; Annie, a black and white tweed suit, Sophie, an oversized coat; the same for Jessie. We were all duly measured for our new clothing, told to return for the first of what would be several fittings, and were shown out of the suite by the dressmaker. I still remember, distinctly, the four of us standing outside in the corridor, looking at each other in horror as it hit us how much we'd spent. In unison we muttered, "What have we done?" I'd spent £62,000—almost a week's salary—which, I later found out, was more than any other Bluebell.

After making our down payments on our new finery, we were all short of cash—me more than anyone else, even though I was the master saver of the group. Earlier that week I'd paid a third of the boat fare for my upcoming passage to Canada, and, in my money lending role, had lent out another £18,000. By the night before payday, I was broke and none of us had money for dinner. Giorgio, Vera's boyfriend, stepped in and bought Jessie and Sophie a meal and the rest of us sat in our room and ate grapes and drank milk, followed quickly by bed and sleep. The sooner we slept, the sooner breakfast would be served.

After enjoying such an enthusiastic audience on opening night, the audiences started to drop off. We quickly concluded that the show was not going to be a success, and one of the girls told me that in the prior year she was on a similar tour that was intended to run for eight months but when it turned out to be a flop it ended after four months. I was also told that if the show was not a success we might immediately be sent on "one-night stands," meaning daily bus rides to towns where we would give one performance only. After a few nights, though, the size of the audiences picked up. The orchestra section of the theater would always be full and the balcony half full, and we routinely danced four *passerellas*. We were told that Marisa del Frate, who was far more popular than Dapporto, was bringing in the crowds.

It was also likely that the Bluebells were responsible for bringing in the crowds. A critic in a magazine wrote, "Dapporto and Marisa del Frate are 'saved' by the Bluebells." Cast members were unhappy about this comment, which momentarily created a bad atmosphere in the theater. Cast members avoided us, and the usual friendly banter was gone. One of the girls, talking to one of the men from the show's vocal quartet, eager to return to the previous friendly atmosphere, went out of her way to tell him, "Sorry. We couldn't help what the critic wrote." "The critic was right," he said, dropping his voice so others couldn't hear.

The critic had been effusive, adding that the Bluebells "looked as though they'd just come out of a beauty salon!" We knew that we looked good on stage and Vera had her eye on each of us new girls to ensure that we were always well turned out. Plus, the costumes helped; bodices were padded as appropriate, and waists were pinched. And attitude? All new Bluebells, and we had been no different, were instructed by their Captain to look out into the auditorium and imagine we were telling each member of the audience, "I've got everything, but you can't have any!"

Occasionally there were famous people in the audience. When this occurred, Dapporto, as he was walking round the *passerella* at the end of the show, would stop the music and introduce the luminary to the audience. A spotlight was put on the celebrity, who then stood up, and everyone in the audience and on the stage applauded until the music started up again and the *passerella* continued. This had occurred three times to date: on the third night, Gia Scala[1] was in the audience.

There were changes at the theater. First, Rita, the assistant choreographer, went back to the States as the show had opened and her work was finished. She dashed into our dressing room to drop off a box of chocolates and say her goodbyes. There were tears in her eyes; it seemed she was trying to avoid breaking down. Had she stayed any longer we would all have been in tears—most of us had grown very fond of her. It was strange to see her in a skirt. We'd never seen her out of blue jeans which, in 1960, weren't worn by mature women.

Lee was still with us for a while longer. He watched the show every night, and gave us a critique, following which, we'd have a rehearsal to fix things he thought needed fixing. Eventually he left the company to return to the States. At the same time, Giorgio, the set designer, left to return to Rome. Vera was in tears, but as we weren't supposed to know that she'd been seeing a member of the company, we had no way of showing her any sympathy, so we didn't.

By then I'd discovered a downside of working in a show: it was very repetitive. One performance was indistinguishable from another, or it was meant to be. Each performance was supposed to be perfect, just as perfect as last night's performance, and that meant that if anything was different from the previous night's performance, something was wrong with one of the performances. Beginning in Milan

---

[1] English-Italian actress; appeared in *The Guns of Navarone* 1962

and throughout the tour, to alleviate the boredom, I would select a "favorite" number, and that would remain my favorite until it was replaced by another. I looked forward to performing that number, because it was my favorite. My energy level would be especially high for that number, because it was my favorite, and performing that number provided a high point for each show, because it was my favorite. I would especially enjoy the music and the costume for that number, and probably as a result of the mind games I gave a better performance, too. I definitely wasn't bored.

I started off with the *Orientale*, because it came after a quick change there was always a degree of relief at having made it on stage in time. Once on stage, the dance was a joy, because it was so different to all our other numbers. Bluebells were ordinarily instructed to smile out at the audience and "show your back teeth," however, in the *Orientale*, we smiled with nary a tooth in sight, just a slight upturn of the ends of a closed mouth. And, if that didn't make it sufficiently different, we danced with bare feet and our legs fully covered!

Now that we had time to relax and enjoy each other's company, I learned that there were basically only three topics of conversation among the Bluebells: men, clothes, and dancing. This wasn't surprising—we were cloistered, with very narrow lives. It was impossible to have a life outside of the theater, the hotel, and Bluebells. We didn't speak or read Italian, we didn't watch TV, we didn't have personal transport, we worked odd hours and had little control over our free time, as a rehearsal could be called suddenly on any afternoon. A few girls occasionally purchased English newspapers, but that's all we learned about the world, and we learned nothing about Italy.

We didn't miss being part of the larger world. We were either teenagers, or barely out of our teens. For myself, I'd spent the last ten months living in London and never once visited a museum. We heard about Khrushchev slamming the table with his shoe at the UN, but that was because he was responding to a speech by Harold MacMillan, so the display had made its way into an English newspaper, but we never heard a whisper about the Bay of Pigs.

Of the three topics I listed above, "men" was the most common, and the discussions generally focused on the lack of integrity to be found in Italian men. When relationships went well, they remained private.

The girls who had relationships within the company didn't discuss them in any detail; not with me, anyway. While I knew a few had very enthusiastic boyfriends in their home-towns, I don't think the girls gave those relationships much thought or attention; but a third classification of boyfriend, those who lived in the city where a girl had recently worked, were more troublesome. It seemed that the girls suffered a lot of heartache with those relationships. In August, upon our arrival in Milan, two of the girls were head over heels in love with boyfriends in Lucerne, where they'd last appeared. For the first six weeks they were continually disappointed, rarely receiving letters from the men, and when the inevitable hap-pened, and letters arrived notifying them of the end of the relationships, many tears flowed.

And then there was Christine, who'd met the love of her life while dancing in Cannes the previous year. She had decided to visit him unannounced at his home in England, and his wife, a wife whose existence of whom Christine had been totally unaware, answered the door. It seemed that most of the girls had gone through one or more painful relationships, and we were all very sympathetic. Christine's relationship even had a special song, "My Funny Valentine." When it came on the radio, our hearts would go out to her, and sixty years later I still find it a very sad song.

We also were in comforter-mode if a girl was on the receiving end of any meanness from another girl. One night at the restaurant, Deanna made a tactless and hurtful comment to Annie about a current boyfriend, a student at the nearby University of Pavia. Annie held back the tears during the meal and during the brief journey up to our room. (The restaurant was on the ground floor of the hotel.) I arrived in the room soon after, and she immediately put her arms around me and sobbed and sobbed. Carol arrived and invited us to Alice and Sophie's room where a group of girls were already analyzing the situation, with Deanna, needless to say, not coming off well! At least six of us ended up in Alice's room, where Annie received lots of comfort and care. She fell asleep in Alice's bed, remaining there the rest of the night, while the rest of us went back to our own beds and by the next day all was forgotten and calm reigned once more.

Carol had an amazing number of male acquaintances she'd met during previous contracts, many of whom would turn up unexpectedly at the stage door after the show, or even at the railway station when we arrived in a city. They'd take a group of us out for a meal and then back to a flat for conversation and music. If Sophie was with us, there would always be a competition amongst the men for her attention. Italian men, at least those with whom we came in contact, were not subtle in their pursuit of a woman, particularly one as appealing as Sophie. I would observe them and wonder why they thought, for one moment, someone as breathtaking as Sophie would give them the time of day. On so many occasions she would merely smile her appealing smile, and the men surrounding her were smitten, and their common sense would fly out the window!

I'm sure the men hoped one or more of us would stay the night, but there was no chance of that. We never had any interest in them beyond conversation and a meal, with the focus on the meal! It was a running joke amongst the girls that the way to win an hour or two of companionship with a group of Bluebells was to offer them a meal.

It was in Milan that I learned that not only can things go wrong during the show, but they can all go wrong in the space of one night.

On one particularly busy night:

- Just prior to the show, Annie had a nosebleed that wouldn't stop.
- Having broken the rules and taken my tights to the hotel to wash them, I promptly left them there.
- During the early part of the Presentation number, while the stage was still in darkness, one of the rods to which the telephones were attached got stuck in the flies.
- A girl in the middle of a heavy period sobbed profusely when we were making the quick change for the

Orientale and, despite Vera's commands, didn't make it on stage.

The mishaps were handled theater style, with no nonsense:
- Annie had cotton wool pushed up her nostril.
- Anna, the show's chief dresser, produced a spare pair of tights.
- The props man rushed past us girls, up the staircase, unhooked the offending rod and jumped down from the highest level of the staircase.
- The doctor was called to the theater.

In the dressing room one evening in mid-October, we were told that Miss Bluebell had phoned just before the show to say two things. One, that the choreographer from the Moulin Rouge in Paris had seen our show the previous Saturday night and had gone back to Paris with the report that we were "wonderful." Second, that night there would be an important journalist out front. An Italian car company was introducing a new model Austin to Italy and wanted us to be used in the publicity. He would be out front to see if we were OK for the job, so, of course, Miss Bluebell wanted us to be our radiant best. After the show that night the journalist appeared backstage and the decision was made that we would be doing the publicity on the coming Friday at 2:30 p.m, and at 6:30 p.m there was to be a cocktail party for "100 personalities." Two of the personalities were to be the actress Pier Angeli and the actor Vittorio Gassman, and twelve of them were to be *"Le Bluebell,"* as we were known in Italy. We were given the option of receiving a gift or money for our services. We responded loudly and in unison, "Money."

On Thursday I got dressed quite early, at 3:30 p.m, because Vera wanted to see what we planned to wear for the cocktail party the next day. I didn't own anything suitable, so Vera had me try on clothes belonging to several of the old Bluebells. A black dress belonging to Kate apparently made me look far too old, so Vera settled on one of Christine's dresses. I don't recall Christine having any choice in the matter, and I remember feeling embarrassed as I wasn't a particular friend of Christine's.

Friday, the day of the event, started early for me with a 9 a.m. trip to the hairdresser. This meant I'd had little sleep, so I started off the day with shadows under my eyes, but I doubt anyone noticed. We'd been directed to have lunch at the hotel restaurant at 12:45 p.m., because there would be no time to eat before the show that night, and we were instructed to only have one or two drinks at the cocktail party, because in the past, girls had fallen off the *passerella* when they'd been drinking beforehand.

At the event, we learned that we were publicizing the amalgamation of the Austin and Innocenti automobile companies and their production of two cars, a new A40 and a sports car. We arrived at the factory, with those of us who'd visited the dressmaker sporting our splendid new outfits, and stood outside on the tarmac while lots of people arrived at the event. We then walked inside, to a very large room and had coffee and cognac. The crowded room included many film stars, the women wearing out-of-this-world outfits. I didn't see Pier Angeli, but Vittorio Gassman was in evidence, as were Josephine Baker and Yvonne Furneux, who'd recently starred in the movie *La Dolce Vita*. We then walked to the factory and were photographed—both still and movie—on cars, around cars, and getting in and out of cars. We affixed smiles to our faces, and there they stayed until the end of the event. It was quite tedious, but an experience I wouldn't have missed. We then went back to our hotel and changed for the cocktail party which was taking place at a high-end hotel. By the end of the day, between the events and the show, we'd made up our faces five times.

When we arrived at the party each woman was given three red roses with stems about two-feet long. That's a long stem to manage, and I lost count of the number of people I stuck with mine, and I had terrible difficulty trying to manage a bag, roses, wineglass, and food. We girls, only twelve of the "one hundred personalities," were joined by lots of businessmen, and I found myself talking to the Export Manager at the Longbridge factory, who lived on the other side of Bromsgrove, close to my home in Birmingham. At the far end of the room there was a car, which you couldn't see in the crowded room until you were on top of it. We headed for it in a tight group, twelve young women who were all somewhere between 5'10" and 6' in our heels. We were quite a sight. Once we reached and surrounded the car, more photos were taken, then we headed back to the theater in the center of Milan, and back to our other lives. A few days later a double-page spread of us at the events was published in *Le Ore* magazine, and a week later, girls who went to the movies to see *Can-Can* saw us in the accompanying newsreel. For our trouble we each were paid £20,000.

The next night Vera gave a speech in the dressing room. The purpose was, I supposed, to share her infinite wisdom, and in doing so to let us know that those of us who treated dancing as a normal job should "get out" quickly. I didn't know if she was addressing me, specifically. Maybe she'd learned that I'd already paid part of my fare to Canada, but I didn't think so. In any case, she certainly succeeded in making me feel guilty. She went on to say that the people she was referring to just do their job, putting in enough effort to get by, and no more. By then I thought I had recognized myself. She ended by saying that these people were dead on stage, and what she liked to see were a few nerves. This last bit cheered me up as I think she'd probably witnessed more nerves in me than in anyone else on the contract. I was left certain only of how much Vera liked the sound of her own voice.

Later that week all the dancers, boys and girls, had a rehearsal. We started at 2 p.m. and the boys came in at 3:30 p.m. to rehearse with us until 4:30 p.m. At 4:45 p.m. we'd finished one dance with the boys and Vera said, "we'll now do the Finale." Luciano said that they'd worked their one hour and they couldn't work longer, or else he'd be tired for the show. He yelled at Vera, Vera yelled back, starting with Italian, giving up and giving him a mouthful of English. Franco (who was on Vera's side of the argument) started to talk to Luciano and that started a fight. Then Jessie burst into tears. Vera then declared the rehearsal closed. We were to have worked until 5 p.m. so we got out a quarter of an hour early. Later that night, flowers and chocolates arrived for Vera and also chocolates for us, from Luciano. One of the other boys told Vera that Luciano had injections each day for "nerves," something to do with his mental health. Maybe this was so, maybe not. Looking back over the nine months, I viewed Luciano as a high-strung, out-going, noisy Italian man; not that different from many other Italians I'd met.

The next night I made a mistake that made a great impression on me—so much so that I'm certain it is the source of the occasional anxiety dreams I had for the following forty years. Going down to the stage for the Sexy Studio number, I was wearing my very pretty black and pink costume. I looked down at my feet and instead of seeing black patent shoes, I was still wearing the white shoes from the previous number. It was unthinkable to have gone on stage wearing the wrong shoes! I immediately raced back up the stairs to the dressing room knowing that I would miss the beginning of the number. I changed my shoes, raced back down to the stage, and waited in the wings until there was a moment in the dance when I could slip, unnoticed, back into line. I was out of breath, adrenalin flowing, and horrified, realizing I'd just broken a cardinal rule: A Bluebell number had begun, and I wasn't on stage.

While I was waiting in the wings, I remember fondly, I found I was surrounded by stagehands and the Stage Manager, all there to give me moral support. They knew I could be in a lot of trouble; to not appear on stage on cue was unforgivable and I would have deserved any and all anger that Vera dished my way. After the number she said very little, and she never raised the issue again. I surmised that as she had seen me hurrying back up the stairs, she knew that I would be missing when the lights went up. Looking back, it seems to me, I've more than paid for my original sin over the last four decades, by waking up suddenly in the night, heart beating fast, finding myself about to go on stage wearing the wrong shoes! There is, indeed, another variant to these anxiety dreams where I am trying to run down a steep narrow staircase to the stage but am not able to pass a hoard of people coming up the stairs, which to my recollection never actually happened. I suspect it merely reflects the stress of repeatedly, narrowly making on-time entrances.

When I arrived on stage for the same number the following night I was in for a bit of teasing, enduring comments like, "Good to see you, Liz," and "See you made it tonight."

A change in my off-stage appearance was permitted by Vera around this time. My hair had naturally become straighter, so I was now wearing it down, rather than pinned up in a French pleat. Everyone liked it better, so I liked it. However, it did mean that I always had to wear rollers in bed, and the only night I could miss was Saturday night, because on Sundays we performed two shows, so I wasn't going to be seen in public—at a restaurant for example—before the first show.

As November approached, the next part of the tour was made known to us. On November 2nd we were to begin two-and-a-half months of traveling throughout northern Italy. We'd spend a week or two each in Torino, Bologna, Genoa, and San Remo, and between these cities we'd be doing one-night stands in smaller towns. By mid-January we'd arrive in Rome.

In the days before the company moved to Torino, we were given instructions on how our luggage was to be handled. Our large, heavy cases were to be at the theatre on Tuesday morning as they were to travel with the wardrobes that carried our costumes. All we were responsible for was to put them outside our hotel room door on Monday night. Smaller suitcases and any that didn't lock were to be kept with us. We spent Monday packing.

CHAPTER SIX

ON THE ROAD, BLUEBELL STYLE

The final performance in Milan revealed a special kind of theater magic. I was accustomed to the precision with which all backstage activity took place during a performance, but now that I was experiencing my first "final performance," I observed this precision taken to rigorous new levels. As each scene ended, the scenery that wasn't needed for a later scene, and the related props, were immediately dismantled and readied for transport to Torino. In our dressing room the same process was repeated. The moment we came off stage our costumes and accessories were taken from us and placed in large traveling wardrobes. The process was so smooth, and I found it fascinating. Throughout the evening our dressing room, which normally was afloat with lace and sequins, became emptier and emptier.

At the end of the evening, we said goodbye to lots of people working at the theater. Prior to this I had no idea that many of the dressers and stagehands we were so familiar with were not part of the permanent company. We girls were sad, but I, personally, was also pleased. We were on the move and I was a little closer to my transatlantic trip.

At the train station a sketch artist we'd befriended at the restaurant in Milan was there to see us off, giving each of us a carnation. Not many of the company were on the train. Those who owned cars (none of us girls, of course) preferred to drive, at least while we were traveling around northern Italy. The journey was uneventful, but eye-opening to a girl traveling abroad for the first time. I saw terraced hillsides for the first time, and laundry hanging from the windows of village homes; touring Italy was going to be fascinating.

I had a corner seat, with Sophie next to me and Jessie opposite. Jessie was eating a pear, with her mouth partially ajar, giving Sophie and me a good view of the chewing process, and we couldn't miss the drips of juice that came rolling down her chin. Sophie was disgusted, and commented, in her broken English, "Oh Jessie, you *devolt* me." Sophie could say anything and sound adorable!

While on the subject of food, I had my first *marron glacé*, a candied chestnut, a specialty of the northern Italian region we were traveling through. (Yes, the French claim them too, but they first gather the chestnuts in the forests of northern Italy, so I'm told.) I recognized luxury; even my tastebuds recognized luxury. A slightly grainy texture, the crunch of sugar and the unique chestnut flavor.

Upon arrival in Torino, we took a taxi from the station and went on to the *pensione*. The *pensione* was beautiful, but there were only three rooms for twelve girls. Vera immediately called the theater to tell them that this wouldn't do. She was told that there was an international exhibition on in Torino and all the hotels were booked, and so we had to stay put. Annie and I were in a room with Alice and Sophie, which was a bit cramped to say the least. Two of the rooms had one double bed plus two bunk beds, while our room had a double bed, a single, and a bed that unfolded from a sideboard, which is where I slept. I'd never seen such a piece of furniture before, let alone slept in one. To add insult to injury, the cost was £1,200 a week, £200 more than our room in Milan. Vera tried to get the owner to bring down her price but wasn't able to budge her.

After having a coffee, we went to the theater, the Alfieri, and had a look around. The scenery and backstage workers had arrived. It was great to see everyone, and it made it seem like home. We had a small meal, took a tram (incredibly brave, considering our minimum mastery of Italian), went to see a Kim Novak and Kirk Douglas movie, back to the *pensione* and then to sleep for twelve hours. The next day we had a rehearsal at 5 p.m. and all looked forward to doing a show that evening; we'd missed it last night! Everyone liked to perform, including me.

In spite of my initial complaints, it turned out that it was rather nice having four in a room. A huge positive of being in a touring show, working and living with eleven girls, was the companionship, which I never failed to enjoy. Vera had warned us that she would "split up friends" if there was too much noise. There was no question that our room was the noisiest, but we somehow got by. My guess is that the *pensione* management didn't complain, and that was all that mattered.

A few days after arriving in Torino I developed a terrible sore throat, which progressed into a bad cold. In 1960 there were no drugs to alleviate the symptoms and, of course, there was no question of having any time off work. Performing on stage with a cold was miserable, and the misery was twofold. First, dancing when only breathing through the mouth isn't very efficient. I became far more winded than I normally would—but maybe that was a reflection of the fact that I was ill, rather than the point of entry of the air! But the second and major problem was the constant wiping of my nose, which would smudge my lipstick. (Stage lips were closer to the nose than regular lips with the two peaks of the cupid's bow being further apart and higher than the natural lip. We would draw the edge of the lip with a red pencil then fill it in with lipstick). The final thing I needed to do before going on stage was to blow my nose, which needed to be followed by a make-up "patch-up." Trouble was, by the time I'd completed the nose-blowing and patch-up, I needed to blow my nose again. We had to look perfect on stage, always.

Dapporto had told several of the girls, "If Torino likes a show the whole of Italy will like the show," so we were eager for Torino to like the show, and very sensitive to any negative reactions from the audience. Unfortunately, unlike those in Milan, the audience just seemed "dead," and didn't react to what we did on stage. We still had full houses, but there was little applause and it made us dancers miserable. In Milan, we always had applause when the fringe curtain went up on our Presentation number, yet we hadn't had applause once in Torino. Admittedly, the curtain had gone up late each time, but that shouldn't have made that much difference. We were still gorgeous, right?

Dapporto, trying to fix the matter, stood in the wings and started clapping. The audience didn't take the hint, though, so the following night he stood out in the auditorium, in the side aisle, and clapped enthusiastically. This time the audience got the idea.

Also, we weren't receiving applause for our Sexy Studio number—at least for the first few shows. The lighting was incredibly important in this number and the timing of the lighting had been wrong on every performance, so maybe the lack of enthusiasm was understandable.

To explain: the scene was a photographic studio. The stage setting was stark. The backdrop was plain white, and on the stage were black wooden platforms and ladders; with arc-lamps on poles, shining down on the stage. When the lighting was correctly timed the scene opened in blackness and then, gradually, to sensual music, the lighting increased to reveal the girls silhouetted in different poses around the stage and on the platforms and ladders, dressed in pink and black lace leotards, with opera-length black lace gloves. The lighting was a subtle shade of pink, and the visual impact of the total scene was very effective, particularly as it came directly after the noisy, garish, Victoria Station scene. Needless to say, when the stage lighting was immediate and not gradual, the audience didn't see a sight worthy of applause, but rather a dozen girls in position, awaiting the beginning of their dance.

The final straw was when we saw the audience walk out of the theater before the end of the show. While we were dancing along the *passerella*, people in the orchestra seats would be walking up the aisles and the people in the gallery were shouting at the attendants to let them out of the theatre. Over dinner (we would all eat at the same restaurant after the show) Dapporto explained the phenomenon to us, "They're leaving the theater early to catch the last tram." So, it wasn't the show, but it was still a bit disconcerting.

The interesting thing was when we entered the theater before the show, we'd see a long queue of people waiting to buy tickets. Unfortunately, not only did they queue to get in, they also queued to get out!

I was reminded of a similar nightly event I'd watched from the stage at the Hanley Theatre Royal, home of the pantomime I'd appeared in several years earlier. At the time, the national anthem was played at the end of the evening, after the audience's applause. Just like the audience in Torino, Hanley audiences wanted to catch the last bus, but if they were anywhere in the auditorium when the "Queen" started they could not escape as it was sacrilege to move a muscle during the national anthem. Night after night, during the applause, members of the audience would head up the aisles only to have their escape cut short by the first notes of the Queen, and so have to remain, frozen-in-place, until the anthem ended, and only then could they complete their get-away.

But I digress: to get back to the applause problem in Torino. Vera announced that we were going to have a rehearsal every day. Ever the pessimist, she also told us to start saving, as it looked as though the show was going to close early!

My cold didn't leave quickly. The two performances on Sunday knocked me out and I was so thankful when the day was over. Vera told me to stay in bed the following day, but, of course, get up for the show. "You've got to sleep because you're working harder than you've ever worked before and your body isn't strong enough for it." I slept until 3 p.m. We'd all had a hard week with three two-show days. Incidentally, we weren't paid a bonus for the additional two-show days, but we were docked for our travel day, when there was no show!

I was now realizing how disadvantaged I was, having no boyfriend in the company. I found out that when we were in Milan some of the girls had been taken to Lake Como, and now I was hearing that the girls were visiting the sights in the greater Torino area, none of which I saw.

About six nights into the run, the Torino audience suddenly warmed to the show. Maybe all the hard-to-please types had come the first few nights. But, as I said, they "warmed": they were not "hot." In Milan, the audience applauded the moment they caught a glimpse of the Bluebells as the fringe curtain lifted. In Torino the fringe curtain went up, no applause; we performed the dressing pantomime, no applause; we walked down the staircase, across the stage and danced round the *passerella* with "spots" on us and, finally, we received applause. Happily, the daily rehearsals that Vera promised us the previous week didn't materialize as the applause was so improved. You might have thought we'd planted friends in the audience!

The big news of the day was a secret. Deanna and Kate were engaged to Delio and Luciano, two of the dancers. Our room found this pretty amusing as, apparently, Deanna and Kate had been "engaged" on every contract they'd been on. Of course, Vera didn't know about these "engagements."

Italian men in general, those we had casual contact with, acted in our minds, like buffoons. They thought they were the most desirable creatures on earth and yet would stoop to any indignity in order to catch a glimpse, maybe, of a girl in a bra or pajamas. We never saw them as frightening, just absurd.

It was 4:30 a.m. on a Sunday morning. Alice was out on a date; Annie and I were in bed. Sophie, wearing a coat over her PJ's, was headed down the corridor to the *pensione* kitchen to leave our breakfast order. She raced back to the room, still holding the list, saying there were men wearing only pajamas in the corridor. We had to get that list to the kitchen, so for the next trip, I joined her. Between us we found the courage! We edged our way down the corridor, but could still hear the men so, again, dived back to our room. We found this incredibly funny, to think we were acting scared of men, in pajamas, in a *pensione* corridor! We tried to stifle the laughter as we didn't want to wake up the whole building but were set off again when we found one of the men had followed us back into the room. He wanted to know what language we spoke, and in return I asked him to take the breakfast list to the kitchen. So, there we were, three girls in rollers, with cream on our faces, wearing coats over our PJs, stifling hysterical laughter at the sight of a man in pajamas, sitting on a bed, holding a breakfast list in one hand, and holding up his PJ trousers (lest they fall down) with the other. We were quite beyond uttering any words such as "get out".

Suddenly the man heard the shuffle of slippers in the corridor and, without a word, dived into the wardrobe. There was a knock on the door. Annie said that it must be Alice, so I went to let her in and found the key had been turned in the lock. Apparently, our visitor had hoped he wouldn't be disturbed. I unlocked the door, and there was Vera, in dressing gown and no make-up, come to see what all the laughter was about. I was unable to speak. Annie pointed limply at the wardrobe and said, "There's a man in the wardrobe!" Vera looked incredulously at her and strode over to the wardrobe, opened the door and was met by the crouching figure of the man in his PJs. Oh, did she yell at him, I assume in Italian. She told him to get out, asked if he thought he was at a Casino, and that we were prostitutes? She followed him back to his room yelling at him all the way, while his roommate (also in PJs) appeared at our door to let us know that their room was just round the corner! "Of all the bloody cheek!" I wrote in my diary.

Christine had pulled a ligament the previous day and did none of the strenuous dances that night. Because she was in the front row, the spacing needed to be changed in nearly every dance. The following afternoon we heard that she was to have three days' complete rest. Alice was Christine's understudy as the ice cream seller in the Victoria Station number, so we had a rehearsal in our room, around the bed. It was definitely more laughter than rehearsal.

Under the best conditions the Victoria Station number was a romp. As the scene opened, the audience saw a stage full of activity. A pantomime of a busy train station followed, with all the dancers on stage except Annie and Alice, who could be heard over the P.A. Annie, in a very plummy voice, announced, "The next train arriving at Platform 2 is the 9:22 from Bognor." Then Alice would break in with "London Bridge, East Croydon, Purley, Purley Oaks to Tunbridge Wells, and Brighton." There was a policeman chasing a thief, a newspaper seller calling out "*News, Star,* and *Standard,*" and an ice cream seller advertising her wares, all in a Cockney accent. And, of course, there was a businessman in a bowler, holding a briefcase and umbrella. When there were English people in the audience, they loved it!

All of the dancers wore several over-garments appropriate to their character. I was one of three schoolgirls with our teacher (played by Vera, of course). We wore wide-brimmed *Gigi*-style school hats (like Leslie Caron wore in the movie of the same name) with pigtails hanging from them, a gray and white cape round our shoulders, white gaiters on our legs and white gloves. At the end of the pantomime section of the scene we all threw off our top layers, leaving all the girls in gray skirts, red jackets nipped in at the waist, and the boys in gray suits. The ensuing dance was tricky: a mazurka, danced in threes, two girls with one boy, and involved dancing in wheel-shaped formations and then peeling off to form other formations.

The first night without Christine was more of a romp than usual. Alice pantomimed the "ice cream seller" beautifully. That left Annie having to do double duty over the P.A., saying her own lines and Alice's. Annie's Cockney rendition was always funny, (her natural accent was broad Yorkshire), but when she was called on to play two characters, the results were even funnier and the dancers on stage broke up with laughter. The on-stage chases that followed then went awry and the wrong people were pushed over at the wrong times. We received lots of applause for the scene, so we weren't the only ones enjoying ourselves.

Earlier in the evening, just before the Presentation number, Vera called my name down the dressing room. Would I be ready, early, for the second number in Act I, the Hyde Park number, as I was doing Christine's part? I went over the steps twice with my new partner, Franco, before we went on. My customary part in this number was a walk-on at the back of the stage after the other girls were already on the stage, so I had no idea what went on earlier in the number when the more experienced dancers were doing their bit. I knew it was not an intricate dance number as the dancers were on stage primarily to provide vocal back-up for Dapporto's solo. Still, I wanted to look good and not let the team down. There was a blackout before the scene and I had assumed that we'd be walking on when the lights went up, but instead we walked out during the blackout (correct that, I was led out during the blackout). We stood back-to-back, alone, front center stage, holding hands and swaying to the music. Franco kept issuing instructions in Italian (not helpful) while I, with a bad case of nerves, clutched his hands, hoping not to injure his fingers. Vera said later that what I did was good. I felt great, and was energized for the whole show.

"*Tutti Inglese*," the dressers, and other Italians in the show, often said of me. Other times they'd say, "You're different from the other Bluebells. When you get off stage, or when you're in a restaurant, instead of gossiping with the other girls you always look straight ahead, always with your own thoughts." I suspected they were confusing shyness with "Englishness."

Even so, I did notice changes in myself. My new self always had sufficient supplies of many of the important commodities in this line of work, including emery boards, cotton wool and postage stamps. Previously I'd been a person who depended on others to make sure I got by. No more. I loved being depended on by the other girls. Maybe I felt it evened things up a little: I may not have been the best dancer, but they could always rely on me, even if only for an emery board.

Meanwhile Sophie and Deanna had been hired for publicity work at the Torino Motor Show. Vera told the rest of us that if we were to attend the Show as guests, we would have to look as good as Sophie and Deanna had looked; we had to "keep up their standard."

Sophie told me that years earlier, her father had paid into a Club at his work for a whole year for the fare and entrance fee for the family to go to the Brussels World Fair in 1958. They entered the Russian Pavilion and Sophie was asked to don a Russian fur coat for a photograph. She was paid for the work on the spot: the equivalent of the amount her father had put away throughout the previous year. She would've been fourteen at the time.

Giorgio, Vera's boyfriend, showed up that night. We saw him as soon as we came off the Sexy Studio number. Vera was happy, and we were happy for her. More to the point, if Vera was happy, then our life would be easier. We hoped that Giorgio would keep Vera occupied so there'd be no rehearsal the following day, but we had no such luck. There was a bright spot to Giorgio's arrival, though. Vera had recently moved into the room next door to ours, and there was no way she'd be using her room that night. We could make noise.

Sylvia had a boyfriend, an *impresario* in his forties, who we considered old. He was charming, had a beautiful car, and, of course, as with most of the Italians we met, a wife. He took Sylvia out every night for dinner in Milan, and now was visiting her in Torino. He was also a pragmatist, and regarding the things we heard about the abbreviated length of the tour, predicted that we would indeed make it to Rome because that was where all the money was to be made.

In the meantime, we were preparing for "one-night stands." We had several rehearsals with the orchestra to rearrange the Presentation number, needed because we wouldn't be doing the "dressing pantomime." We'd start the number wearing the complete costume, so cuts had been made to the music. Incidentally, Vera told me around this time my dancing was getting stronger, which I took to mean that I was no longer conspicuous as an inexperienced dancer. So, I'd received a compliment from Vera. Good.

On the last day we spent in our foursome room, Sophie, Alice, Annie, and I were relaxing on our beds listening to ballet music on the radio, all of us stiff after the recent rehearsals. Sophie, never inactive for long, mimicked a ballet mistress working her class very hard. The music changed to a Granados *Spanish Dance* and she grabbed her castanets. The music changed once more and she and Alice moved on to a performance of a *pas-de-deux* between the beds, with Sophie, for some reason, and of course looking adorable, wearing a pair of pale blue lace bikini briefs on her head.

We would leave Torino the next day and were told to pack our rehearsal gear in our large suitcases which we wouldn't see again until we reached Bologna. This meant we would only have light rehearsals until we arrived there on November 23rd, which was good news.

Our last performance in Torino was wild, with lots of students in the audience, blowing noisy whistles. The reaction among the *Torinese* was baffling: the girls were popular and were cheered, while the boys and male actors were cat-called and jeered at.

Christine, who still wasn't dancing in the show, was assigned by Vera to watch the show and give criticism to those girls that needed it. She had never been a Captain, but she was a very experienced dancer, so her critique had weight. My advice from her was that I "needed a bomb behind me." This, she unhelpfully explained, was due to the fact that I'd received no dance training. It's not encouraging to be told you're not giving your all. I would just continue to do my best.

CHAPTER SEVEN

WE NEXT PLAY CREMONA, THEN ON TO VERONA

And so we started out on our first group of one-night stands. We traveled to Biella, Brescia (two days), Cremona and Mantova, ending up in Bologna. Each town was a two to three hour's train journey from the last. We'd meet at the station around noon, arrive at our destination between 3 p.m. and 4 p.m., make a visit to our hotel, have a meal, and then meet at the theater for a 7 p.m. rehearsal before the show.

These rehearsals were extremely important. We learned modifications to the dances that Vera would devise so we could perform them on a stage that might be a completely different size or shape to the one we'd danced on the previous night. For example, with a smaller or narrower stage, Vera would figure out if the dancers had to work closer to each other, and how much closer. She would give a few dancers in the front row points of reference, the last seat next to an aisle for instance, and they would make sure that they were directly in front of those points at certain moments in the dance. The other dancers would then figure out where they should stand or dance relative to that dancer. The system seemed to work.

We all, including me, quickly found that one-night stands produced a cashflow problem. Suddenly we had to pay our hotel bills on a daily basis. We'd been accustomed to paying a weekly bill on payday, when we had an abundance of cash. The immediate problem was that we'd used our last payday's cash to pay the Torino *pensione*, but now had to come up with serious money every day. Yes, I know, I said I always had excess cash but by now I'd not only paid a deposit on my fare to Canada, but I'd also purchased skis for my boyfriend. A Christmas gift, they were Corvina laminated hickory, steel-edged skis—highly prized at the time. Supposedly they were very expensive to purchase in Canada, but not so if purchased in Italy and then shipped to Canada as a gift.

The one-night stand audiences were good. The local citizenry appreciated that we had brought our show to their town. For us it was tiring, because we didn't get enough sleep. We were accustomed to a 1 p.m. wake-up call, but during one-night stands we had to be at the train station at noon, having already packed and checked out of the hotel by that hour.

Vera had hinted that the color of my hair needed changing. Now she was hinting no more; I couldn't ignore her any longer. The day we arrived in Bologna we didn't have a show—it was a travel day. I went to the hairdressers to have the color of my hair changed and became a blonde. It made me look quite different: my eyes looked darker and my skin less pale. Even though it was far blonder than I expected, Vera thought it should be lighter. It was still rather mousy, according to her.

Meanwhile, upon arrival in Bologna I found a telephone message waiting for me. I was intrigued, fascinated, all of the above, and quickly returned the call. I was rather hoping that some facet of my Bluebell appeal had preceded my arrival in Bologna. *This must be what it was like to be a real Bluebell Girl!* I thought. Instead, I was disappointed to learn that a group of American medical students who had dated the girls the previous year wanted to take us out. They'd got my name off the show poster! In a slew of phone calls, they invited us to join them at a party. Vera wisely said, "no," because we didn't know them, which I explained to the men. It didn't end the phone calls, but we didn't meet them, and we didn't attend their party.

At this time, I received a rather mean, seven-page letter from my mother. She was taking this last opportunity, before I turned twenty-one (the next day), to let me know what a selfish person I was. I won't relay the sad details, but needless to say I was upset, so I shared the letter with Vera. She thought they were the words of a jealous woman. Maybe she was right, but I didn't think so. In discussing the letter, I also divulged my plan to go to Canada at the end of the contract. I was sure Vera would share this information with Mr. Libo, as he was about to visit. This outcome I regretted as I wanted him to continue to treat me as equal to the other dancers. I reasoned that, once he knew I wouldn't be available for additional contracts, he'd have no interest in me. Regardless of the outcome, for the moment it helped to talk to Vera, so you can add "therapist" to the job description of the Bluebell Captain. I'm sure she wasn't paid nearly enough!

The letter was soon forgotten because a mystery was brewing. Mr. Libo and Penny, the Captain of a troupe that'd been working in Glasgow, were arriving the next day. The Glasgow troupe was on vacation before they opened in

Manchester, and the word was that Penny was coming to take the place of Christine while she was giving her leg total rest. This news sounded very odd to everyone as that would leave our troupe with two Captains. Furthermore, Penny had been the Captain of the Bluebells in the previous year's Dapporto tour, when there was so much trouble, resulting in three girls getting fired. Vera told us that she thought that maybe Penny had been sent to spy on our troupe!

The following day, November 26, would be my twenty-first birthday. On the 25th, Penny arrived but there was no sign of Mr. Libo. We learned that she was not there to take Christine's place but to "see how things were going." That sounded to me like spying. The mystery thickened. We were later told that the purpose of her visit was to investigate an incident from last year's Dapporto tour, when she'd been the Captain. Apparently, one of the girls had been hospitalized and was now suing the Bluebell organization because she had been "neglected and ill-treated," and she'd come to Bologna to talk to members of the company (actors and singers) who'd all been in last year's show, to "find out about things." Vera wasn't happy about any of this. She told one of the girls that as our troupe seemed happy and there'd been no trouble—whatever that meant—Mr. Libo probably thought there was something "fishy" going on, hence he felt compelled to investigate.

The only thing we knew was that three of the girls were fired at the end of the contract for "socializing" with members of the company, and that Anselmo, a member of the vocal quartet, had told the company Director that the quartet would walk out if any of last year's girls worked in this year's show. Now one of those girls was suing Miss Bluebell. What had really gone on, I would never know.

That afternoon we went to another theater in Bologna where the Paul Steffen Dancers were appearing. Paul Steffen was a choreographer of international renown and his dancers were exciting to watch. We sat in the stalls and watched a rehearsal, enthralled, knowing that we were fortunate to have this opportunity to see them; we were so inspired that we returned to the theater and practiced before our show even though a rehearsal hadn't been called.

After the clock struck midnight during the show, many cast members wished me a happy birthday, both on stage (surreptitiously, out of the corner of their mouths) and off. After the show, all the girls met in our room and joined Annie and me for *panettone* and *spumoni*. I received the traditional Bluebell's twenty-first birthday gift, a gold charm bracelet (with no charms on it at this point). The bracelet was very substantial, and I was instructed to only add a few large charms. (If Vera could see it now, she would not give it her nod of approval; it's jammed full of charms big and small, received as gifts through the ensuing sixty years.) From Vera I received a silk scarf that matched my new coat, and a writing case from Annie. It was my first experience, ever, of hosting an event: a dozen noisy girls in robes, sprawled around the bed and chairs in the room. It was a very nice birthday celebration, and I couldn't have asked for anything better.

My mother, apparently now beyond the momentary dissatisfaction that led to her critical birthday letter, had organized a "card-send" from my hometown, resulting in my receiving fifty cards. She also, somehow, managed to get my father to write me a letter. I'd never received one from him before so I didn't recognize his writing! He was a witty man and the update he gave on the health of his elderly father-in-law, whom he didn't like, was typical: "Grandpa is still struggling. Heaven doesn't seem to beckon, and no-one will give him a push." My mother, with not a witty bone in her body, had sent me a box of a hundred photoslides of family and friends and views of my hometown—which I thought a very nice idea.

We discovered that Mr. Libo had arrived when we saw him in the audience, sitting with Penny. He watched a matinee and then in the evening went to see the show in which the Paul Steffen Dancers were appearing. I had now met Penny. She appeared to be a nice woman; wore a business suit and spectacles and looked like a "boss's secretary." It was interesting to meet another Captain. Interestingly, within two hours of arriving in Bologna she had found out that two of the girls were dating members of the company! The number was a little low, but so much for secrecy!

We learned that Christine had four more days of treatment and if that didn't improve her knee, she would be going home for an operation to repair a torn meniscus, and that Mr. Libo had a girl ready to send out to Italy to replace her.

With Penny's arrival, we girls in the troupe became Vera's greatest supporters. Although as a group we didn't discuss it, it was obvious that having a second Captain in her territory put Vera in an uncomfortable position. No longer were we eleven girls and a Captain, who we rarely had anything nice to say about; we were a troupe of twelve girls. There was no splitting us.

Ian, my boyfriend, had sent me money for my birthday. He wanted me to buy clothes and where better than Italy to buy them. Vera, always ready to help us with our appearance, came with me. I dragged her into many, many stores and together we selected a deep red woolen jersey suit and a beautiful chunky, crystal necklace. A day later, when I picked up the suit after alterations had been made, I modeled it and everyone said that, without a doubt, I now looked like a Bluebell.

The next day Mr. Libo gave his critiques to Vera. He told her I had improved a lot! Later he came to the dressing room. He wanted to see some of the girls at the hotel the next day and he worked his way down the dressing room table identifying those he would be seeing; Monica at 3:30 p.m., Jessie at 4 p.m. I was next along the table, so I held my breath, but was not mentioned. Then Deanna was called for 4:30 p.m. As Mr. Libo never said "well done" to anyone, I was thrilled to not have my name mentioned. In hindsight, it was probably a reflection of Vera having told him I was going to Canada.

Penny left the next morning. Mr. Libo said she only came on a social call as she was visiting a friend in Milan. Hmm!

The girls were secretly, or maybe not so secretly, sharing their rooms with male members of the company. Christine's room was next to ours. Her boyfriend, one of the actors, had a cough and Annie and I heard the cough all night. It seemed that when the company was in the same hotel as us, there was much room-sharing, not unexpected at all.

Mr. Libo returned to Paris, but before leaving he walked round the dressing room making comments to girls, this time including me. He told me I'd improved a lot but that I was too thin. He told Annie she was too short, as she was only just about 5'7". (I don't know what she was supposed to do about that.) He told Jessie (and repeated it to Vera) she was "letting the troupe down" with her balloon-shaped face and the peculiar expressions she pulled with it. Annie was disheartened when she heard his comments and I'm sure Jessie was too, but she didn't talk to me about it. I was just relieved that he thought that I was making the Bluebell standard.

Later, Christine shared with me that he had told her that I "could work harder." This was probably true, but it seemed to me that Christine enjoyed giving me news that would hurt my feelings. Maybe she would be replaced by someone a little friendlier. I think possibly that she, as a good dancer, was disappointed that Miss Bluebell hired girls with as little dance background as me, as it couldn't help but bring down the level of performance on stage. Or maybe she just didn't like me.

The next day we were on our way again. Nine more one-night stands before we reached Genoa. Do you remember that song from *Kiss Me Kate*? (Thank you, Cole Porter.)

> *We open in Venice,*
> *We next play Verona,*
> *Then on to Cremona.*
> *Lotsa quail in Cremona.*
> *Our next jump is Parma,*
> *That heartless, tartless menace,*
> *Then Mantua, then Padua,*
> *Then we open again, where?*
> *In Venice.*

We sang it often. It was us. We were hitting the towns in a different order, but it was us! Vera had a great voice and had appeared in a production of *Kiss Me Kate*, so in the dressing room would belt out many of the songs, with us joining in. We loved it.

We left Christine in Bologna. She had her last treatment that morning, and in the evening was on her way home to England. Unfortunately, her large suitcases, with all her clothes, had gone with all our suitcases to Genoa. They'd catch up with her later.

It was a tiring two weeks, reminiscent of the last week of rehearsals. Lots of good humor, slightly irrational arguments and not enough sleep. Christine's replacement, Jenny, arrived within a few days, and she had to learn the dances quickly. That meant that we had full rehearsals every day (not just walk-throughs in street clothes), regardless of how early we'd been up in the morning for train-call.

Jenny met us in Treviso. She was nineteen and came from Uxbridge, outside London. She was an experienced Bluebell, having just completed a contract in Las Vegas. The show's management wanted her to be in all the numbers by the time we reached Genoa, but that turned out to be wishful thinking. When travel arrangements allowed, she would rehearse with Vera early in the day and we would all meet for a rehearsal later, after we'd arrived in the new city. I knew that picking up dance-steps quickly is what professional dancers do, but I was impressed. She became part of the show quickly, and two days after she arrived, she went on for the first time, in the Salvation Army Parade (an easy, straight-forward number), and also danced the *Passerellas* at the end of Act. I. However, rehearsal time is scarce when you're in the midst of one-night stands, so she wasn't on stage in all the Bluebell numbers until after we arrived in Genoa.

While we Bluebells were working hard to integrate Jenny into the show, we performed a show in Moderna that was a special evening for Dapporto. Twenty-five years earlier he had begun his stage career in that very theater. His original leading lady was there, now a plump, middle-aged, still very attractive woman. And to celebrate the occasion, there were lots and lots of single stemmed flowers attached to the front of the boxes, and the edges of both the *passerella*, and the stage. By the time we began the Hyde Park scene, most of the flowers around the *passarella* had been thrown onto the stage, and we were sitting in a meadow! Franco decided to incorporate the surrounding flowers into the number. He first handed me a carnation, then took another one and throughout Dapporto's song, pulled all the petals off, one by one.

In Pordenone, Enzo (who'd been Christine's boyfriend, the one with a cough) was rushed to hospital. There was an issue with his heart, and his wife was sent for. In the show he played "Johnny the gangster," not a large part, but important to the show's plot (such as it was). There was no understudy, so a man named Calagaris, a business associate of Dapporto often seen hanging around the theater, did the honors. He was not exactly a believable substitute. He was obese and around sixty, while Enzo was in his late thirties—tall, dark, and handsome. Anyway, he studied the lines and got by with help from the rest of the cast. The next night a replacement actor appeared backstage, learned his lines, and went on, and remained with the show until Enzo recovered.

Mysteriously, there were Americans *everywhere* in Pordenone. There were families in our hotel, servicemen in the audience (that should've been a clue), and teenagers at the station and on the train. It is only now that I find out that there was, and still is, a large U.S. Air Force base in the Pordenone area. (My British education had included nothing concerning the role played by the U.S. in rebuilding post-WWII Europe, and in Europe's defense against the Soviet Union.)

Near the end of one-night stands, Marisa, the leading lady had suffered, so it seemed to us, a minor mental or physical breakdown and was unable to work. We assumed it was related to the stress of one-night stands. For a couple of nights we didn't know if she'd be on stage for a number or not. On the first of the two nights in question, the show was an hour late starting and when Marisa eventually arrived on stage she appeared, to us, to be somewhat doped. The following night, in a scene where she would normally stand alone on stage extolling (in song) the virtues of the Prince, then was joined on stage by us, first in conversation and then in song, things didn't go as planned.

We walked on stage and Marisa wasn't there. There was no music, only silence, so we chatted together, none of us knowing how we were going to extricate ourselves from this messy situation. We were shocked into action as the Orchestra Director started up the song at an ultra-*fortissimo* level. We reacted as he hoped, by immediately singing. We had been rescued from our tight spot, but back in the dressing room, we just rolled our eyes, wondering if the audience had any idea what the scene was about: first, twelve girls

chatting together in unintelligible Italian, followed by singing, drowned out by the orchestra, in equally unintelligible
Italian.

On one-night stands, things had a tendency to go wrong
on stage even if all the cast were present. The backstage
workers were incredibly tired, getting far less sleep than the
dancers, so in reality, it was surprising that things ran as
smoothly as they did. Some scenes in the show fared worse
than others. Maybe a particular piece of scenery was too big
for some of the theaters, maybe the electrical requirements
were too complicated, but whatever the cause, the unwritten
objective of everyone on stage was to ensure that the audience wouldn't notice; the performers had to appear oblivious
to the tree that, for some odd reason, was now growing in the
Prince's bedroom!

In Treviso there was a scenery problem. The scheduled
blackout at the beginning of the Hyde Park scene lasted for
around five minutes because the scenery wasn't in place.
When the lights eventually went up, there were trees around
the sides of the stage, and the antique gas lamps in place, but
there was also an enormous gold fan standing at the back of
the stage! It was there ready for the next number, the *Orientale*. The "house" that normally stood in front of the fan,
hiding it from the audience, was missing—maybe it was still
in the truck. Jenny, a Londoner, was sitting in the audience
that night, and later commented that it did seem a little odd
to see a large gold fan standing in the middle of Hyde Park.

In Moderna, where Dapporto had his twenty-fifth show-
business anniversary, there had been a few electrical problems.
The theater hadn't been used for live performances for a long

time, only to show movies, so the mechanics were a bit creaky. First, the lights went off a couple of times in the dressing room and, as sorting costume-pieces in pitch-black is a challenge, Deanna arrived on stage for the Hyde Park scene in white gloves instead of the required yellow. It turned out it didn't matter too much because the stage lights proceeded to fade, and the antique gas lamps completely quit working. The only light on stage was the "spot" on Dapporto. As luck would have it, it was a night scene, so the audience was probably happily ignorant of any problems.

As Jenny learned the dances and performed in the show, she no longer sat in the audience, but instead, sat in the dressing room where she sat next to me. We chatted and I heard all about life in Las Vegas and what it was like, working at the Stardust Casino. She told me that out of twenty-eight dancers and showgirls, sixteen got married and about nine of those marriages were to members of the company. Seems it was easier to break the rules when you were further from Paris. I heard about the Stardust's amazing stage. It had the capability to be a stage, ice skating surface, or swimming pool. And, of course, I heard about the high salary. Overall, she loved the experience. By the way, she told me that when she arrived, she had thought that I was the youngest Bluebell!

The stages we performed on throughout Italy came in all shapes and sizes. Some were so small that, dancing at full speed, you'd find yourself in the opposite wing when that wasn't the intent. Dressing rooms also came in all shapes and sizes. There were good dressing rooms, those that were close to the stage and well-lit, and not such good dressing rooms, those that were miles from the stage, with many failings.

The worst we came across on the whole tour was in Vicenza. It was below the stage, tiny, and the walls were covered in sacking. It felt like we were dressing in a cattle-truck and were convinced that the sacking was placed there to provide housing for fleas. And to top it off there was no water available, so we had to do make-up at the hotel. That night, doing make-up and hair at the hotel, Annie and I completely lost track of time, and suddenly realized it was five minutes to showtime. In full stage make-up and with our chignons piled high, we raced to the theater. When we arrived, the foyer was crowded with people who didn't want to miss the beginning of the show! We tried to push our way through. It didn't work; no one would let us through. So, we did what we thought we had to do, and yelled out (in English), "If you don't let us through, there'll be no show," which got their attention.

We'd been told that the show couldn't travel to Venice because of the difficulty of transporting scenery on the canals so, when we appeared in Mestre, less than six miles from Venice, and were to be there a full day, we took the opportunity to visit Venice. We had to be back at the theatre for a mid-afternoon rehearsal, so we set out really early, after getting only three-and-a-half hours of sleep—not the ideal conditions under which to see this lovely city. We toured the Basilica San Marco and the Doge's Palace, and I made sure that I checked out the Pala d'Oro, a bejeweled altarpiece in the Basilica that I'd been told was a "must see" by one of my mother's friends. It was off-season so the city was deserted, and for the most part, the only tourists we bumped into were members of our company.

While we were in Venice, Jessie and I visited the British Consulate. Periodically, throughout the contract, Jessie needed to check in at a British Consulate to demonstrate that she was alive and well. This was required because she was under the age of eighteen, a British subject and employed abroad, (referred to as being "under license"). She also had restrictions placed on her off-stage life, such as being closely chaperoned at all times. (This was a nice sentiment but pretty impractical when you're one of twelve girls, when the other eleven are not living under such restrictions. Vera did her best.) When we arrived at the Consulate the gates were locked. Jessie pressed the bell and the gate, like something out of a movie, unlocked by a mechanism in the house some distance away. Having never witnessed such a thing before, we thought it astonishing.

Next, we visited some especially beautiful towns. Verona was a wonder! The moment we arrived I went out alone to see the sights. First, I found the Montague home, and then the Capulet's. I went inside, then upstairs into Juliet's room and looked out over the balcony (which I've since learned wasn't her balcony, but there can be happiness in ignorance). Much later, after the show, at 3 a.m., I took a second tour; Dapporto insisted on walking a group of us round the town, pointing out the architectural highlights.

In Padua I got stuck in a lift. Not a good thing to happen at 3 o'clock in the morning. Carol and I had got into one of the two hotel lifts. There were two open, parallel shafts, each with a cage and creaky, cranky, machinery. The lift lurched its way to the second floor where Carol got out. Then, with many jiggles of the gate's closing mechanism, I persuaded it to start up again. It lurched its way upward but came to a stop between floors. No way was it going to move up or down and the alarm didn't work, even when prodded with a hairpin. I thought of climbing out, but that seemed a really bad idea, because if I made a misstep, it was quite a drop. Just when I was thinking that sleeping in the lift wouldn't be the worst thing that ever happened to me, Sophie, Alice, Gabriele, and Delio arrived at the second floor in the second lift. The cavalry had arrived!

Unfortunately, just like the rest of us, they were extremely sleep deprived, with judgment regarding life's little calamities, somewhat off. The sight of me above them, marooned in a cage, caused them to double over in laughter. They found it so funny that tears came to their eyes! Eventually, the laughter subsided, and only then did they realize that I needed rescuing. First, they encouraged me to jump into their arms, but I was having none of that. It seemed a very risky proposition. Eventually, common sense won the day and Gabriele climbed up and handed me down to Delio and, right at that time, Vera emerged onto the landing above, wanting to know what all the noise was about, acting the grumpy parent as ever. She did not find the scene amusing!

Also in Padua, Jessie and I, ever the intrepid tourists, didn't want to miss the important sights. We didn't have a guidebook so we checked at the hotel reception desk, who sent us off on a city bus to see the Basilica of Saint Anthony. We took this trip on the day we left, before train-call at 12:30 p.m., which was very nervy of us.

Looking back on this group of one-night stands I'm amazed we did so much on such little sleep. Considering how tired we must have been we remained amazingly good humored. We all loved traveling and dancing, which probably helped. Of course, if we were traveling, which was most days, we would nap on the train, and I know at least once, before going on for the *Finalissimo*, I leaned against scenery and closed my eyes— a small thing, a bit risky, and probably against the rules. Annie told me that when we eventually got to bed, I'd fall asleep during a conversation. I like to think I got much more efficient at using the hours I was in bed.

August 13, 1960

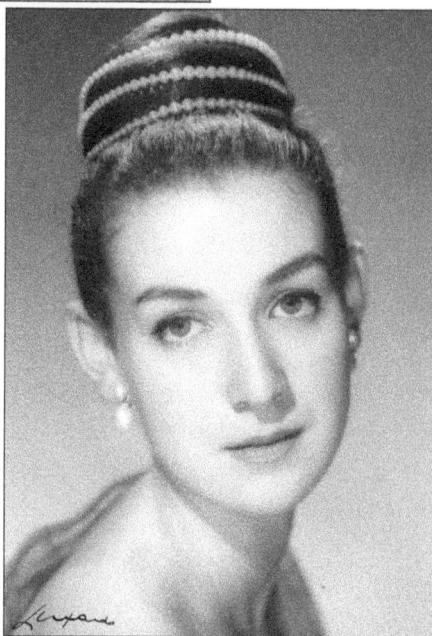

September 19, 1960

photo credit: Elio Luxardo

Teatro Sistina, Rome. Dressing room: Me, "Sylvia" and "Jennie" in our Presentation costumes.

Photo credit: M. Dale, 1961, personal collection of author

*Teatro Sistina, Rome. Dressing room: L-R: Me and "Jennie" in our
Sexy Studio costumes*

Photo credit: M. Dale, 1961, personal collection of author

*Teatro Sistina, Roma. Dressing Room: L-R: Me in my Act I
Finale costume, with Annette, the Bluebell Girls' dresser.*

Photo credit: M. Dale, 1961, personal collection of author

Stadio San Martino, Genoa: posing before the start of the charity bicycle race. L-R: "Sophie", "Deanna", "Jessie", me, "Jennie" and "Kate"

Photo credit: Oggie Magazine

Teatro Sistina, Rome. Dressing Room. The "Senate" L-R: me, "Sylvia", "Jennie" and "Kate"

Photo credit: M. Dale, 1961, personal collection of author

Our Pensione in Rome. L-R: me and "Annie" in our room.

Photo credit: M. Dale, 1961, personal collection of author

In front of the Teatro Sociale, Biella, the location
of the show's first one-night stand.
We posed by the show's poster while "Vera" took our photo.

Photo credit: personal collection of author

CHAPTER EIGHT

GENOA

W e were to be in Genoa for two weeks, spending both Christmas and New Year there. Annie's and my room at the *pensione* had two beds in it, a double and a single. Jessie would be joining us. When the three of us arrived in the room Annie immediately took stock of the situation and claimed the single bed, leaving me to share a bed with Jessie. Now, I got along really well with Jessie, but I didn't want to share a bed with her. Jessie wasn't known for her scrupulous washing habits. The dressers were forever complaining because the insides of her costumes were always dirtier than the insides of the rest of the girls' costumes.

I was horrified and could only glare at Annie to express my disbelief and unhappiness, but I wasn't about to say anything and hurt Jessie's feelings, and the moment passed. When you live so closely with a group of people you let things pass, and Jessie had Vera on her back so much of the time, I wasn't going to add to it.

Waking up from our first night of this new sleeping arrangement we were met with a surprise. The waiter brought in our breakfast. The room was huge; the bed Jessie and I shared was near the door, and Annie's bed was on the far side. The waiter put the tray down on our bed and we watched, thinking he would carry Annie's coffee over to her. Instead, he walked over to her bed, picked up one end and dragged it over to our bed. I assume she was awake.

Marisa, the female star of the show, who'd had a breakdown during one-night stands, was still out of the show. Other female cast members were covering for her, doing "double duty," singing one of Marisa's songs in addition to their own. To me this seemed bizarre; how could an audience follow a plot line if the heroine is played by a different actress in each scene? Fortunately, a couple of days later Marisa returned in good health.

With one-night stands over for a while, we worked on getting rested, but Vera's mood wasn't so easily fixed. She admitted to one of the girls that she kept shouting at people but didn't know why. She was continuously unpleasant to some of the girls, and to the rest of us, even the most benign comment could still be construed as offensive. She was easy not to like.

She was an experienced Captain, so was accustomed to having the responsibility of leading a troupe, but she'd never figured out that the job might be easier if she were more pleasant. Even her acts of generosity were demeaned by the old Bluebells, who'd worked under her previously. She spent hours with me, improving my look both on and off stage, and following me from store to store helping me make my clothing purchases, but the old girls quickly assured me, in a slightly jeering tone, "she only does it because she wants to be known to have the best Bluebell troupe." To me, that seemed a good enough reason.

As I said, she had a huge responsibility, and she took it very seriously. If a Captain didn't do her job, and the

Bluebells didn't produce the Bluebell mystique and allure every time they went on stage, it was doubtful whether an annual show, such as the *Dapporto Spettacolo,* would be hiring them the following year. Her only inducement to keep the girls in line, ensuring they obeyed the Bluebell rules, was to appeal to their pride in being Bluebell Girls.

Maybe she didn't get enough support from Paris. Did she have the equivalent of an HR Department to help her if she had a problem with the employees? The "no fraternization" rule made her the enemy, to be sure, a difficult position for her to be in. From my vantage point, with a few changes, she could've been more successful. Maybe if she'd had a sense of humor. Maybe if she'd thought to compliment the group now and then.

Christmas was nearly upon us and we did our best to make it feel like the holidays, even though we were going to be putting in long hours at the theater. Each of us would be giving—and receiving—three gifts. First, we drew, in secret, for a Bluebell's name and our gift was to be from "The Bluebells" and our identity was not to be disclosed. Then we drew the name of someone in the company (I drew a member of the orchestra), and finally, the most significant, a gift for our roommate.

I was intent on buying Annie a really nice gift. I'd purchased two small practical items and intended to also give her a "luxury" gift, a cigarette case, and it had to be red leather. I found a lovely one, so took it home to fill with the cigarettes I'd also purchased. Only then did I realize there was a problem. It wouldn't take king size cigarettes. Out I went to change it. The shop was a long way from the *pensione,* and when I arrived, they told me that they only changed purchases in the mornings. I pointed out that I slept all morning and decided to just stand there until they served me. It worked. I changed the case for a larger one, but I knew it would still not be large enough. In another shop I found yet another case, just the right size, but not as elegant as the first. There was no returning purchases in 1960, so I ended up with two. I came back to the *pensione* and met Carol who offered to buy the first case from me, and also suggested I try Kent cigarettes in the second, which were a bit shorter than king size, and a cigarette Annie sometimes smoked. They fit. Annie would have to stop smoking king size cigarettes. (Incidentally, Annie hardly smoked when she arrived and now smoked forty cigarettes a day. And, while on the subject of "smoking," only three of the girls were non-smokers.)

I was still not quite ready for Christmas. I still had to get Annie's initials engraved on the case when we received the news that, a couple of days after Christmas, December 27th, there was to be a charity soccer match between the men in the company and the journalists of Genoa and, at the same event, the Bluebells would cycle around the track that encircled the soccer pitch.

Proceeds from this event were to go towards a cancer fund and the event would be filmed for TV and movie newsreels: good publicity for the Bluebells and the show. Within the next few days, we were to go to a journalist's office to try on the clothing we'd be wearing for the event. That visit was abruptly called off when Vera found out the event organizers planned on us wearing football shorts. Vera told Giancarlo, an agent who was our liaison to the event, that that was impossible! He then came up with the bright idea that Anna (the chief dresser at the theatre) could take them in so they'd look more attractive, to which Vera said, "No, she can't!"

Eventually it was agreed that we would wear opaque, black tights, pale blue woolen sweaters and black flat shoes. We would also wear chignons, which was a great relief to me. With any other hairstyle I pictured my hair becoming one large ball of frizz! Once the Vera-approved clothing was available, we went to the journalist's office to try it on, and on the way back Jessie and I called in at the British Consulate. She made her periodic check-in and we made inquiries regarding the date and time of the Christmas carol services at the English-speaking church, All Saints' Anglican.

My life had become easier by then because, due to my incessant letter-writing, everyone knew I was going to Canada, and that there was a boyfriend involved. Generally, this resulted in the men in the company not paying much attention to me. It meant I could be friendly with them and they wouldn't descend to their normal predatory behavior. But there *were* exceptions. It hadn't stopped Guido, a member of the quartet, from inviting me to his room, even though he was well aware that I knew that he was regularly sleeping with one of the other girls. Throughout the nine months, the chutzpah demonstrated by Italian men never failed to astound me. In this particular case it seemed that he was attempting to line me up as a back-up for the time when the relationship with his favorite Bluebell went sour. I was glad when his wife arrived for the Christmas celebration and he had to back off everyone.

Kate's mother and brother arrived for the holidays. Her mother was titled—her formal name was "Lady something," and she and Kate's brother were on their way to purchase a house in the south of France. I was very impressed, and it made me very nervous when I had to speak to her, so I didn't. One evening I was told that she had chocolates for us, we just had to go out to her in the corridor, and she would give us each one. I went without the chocolate rather than approach a Lady. But I didn't go without completely—I joined with the other girls when she brought out the Mars Bars and English Christmas cake she'd carried from England to remind us of home.

Not pertaining to the holidays, but still notable, one of the girls received mail from a friend living in France. It had been addressed to her, % Bluebell Girls, Teatro Margharita, Geneva, Switzerland and had been delivered directly to her at the Teatro Margharita, Genoa, Italy. I couldn't help but wonder whether Europe was just a very small place or if the Bluebells were so famous that they could be readily located. Maybe it was general knowledge in the postal service that there was no Teatro Margharita in Geneva!

Keeping in the Christmas spirit, we spruced up our room, making it the Christmas room. First, we tidied, then added a small tree and later, red and green ribbons around the mirrors. It was always the center of activity, and consequently received the most visits from Vera admonishing us to quiet down.

We also wanted to make our dressing room more festive, but it was messy enough as it was: ten costumes and five pairs of shoes for each of twelve girls (that's a 120 costumes and sixty pairs of shoes, by my reckoning) left no space for anything decorative. We were pleased to see a tall, decorated tree appear outside our dressing room, and also, we'd all contributed to some decorations in one of the actresses' dressing rooms so, all in all, backstage had a festive tone.

On December 23rd, I was still working on my Christmas shopping. I dropped off Annie's cigarette case with an engraver who would inscribe her initials and have it ready to be picked up on the following day, Christmas Eve, when Christmas gifts were to be exchanged. Then I tackled getting a handle on my handbag fixed. I first went to a place that sold leather and other bits and pieces where a very short man offered to take me to a handbag factory. I was surprised at the suggestion, but why not? With difficulty, I followed him along narrow streets. There were hordes of Christmas shoppers and I kept losing sight of him. He led me to an archway, pointed through it, and left. I had no idea where I was, other than I was standing alone under an archway. I asked a man in the crowd for directions to the handbag factory and, lo and behold, after following his directions, I found myself inside a handbag factory, and, yes, there and then they mended my handbag for me!

We had a busy Christmas Eve. We were to meet at the theater to take taxis out to the stadium where we'd have a rehearsal for the cycling event and have publicity photos taken to appear in the local newspapers. I was ten minutes late and got a lecture from Vera: "If everyone else took as little interest in publicity work as you do ..." Giancarlo, the agent, took forever to find taxis for us, but eventually we arrived at the stadium, where the men were already practicing for the soccer match. We then learned what was expected from us. It was to be a race! Vera was mad when she heard this. It wasn't her idea of Bluebell publicity (nor ours, for that matter). The plan was for us to cycle around the track two-and-a-half times, the winner to be given a cup of flowers (or some such thing), and then we'd wave while we cycled the last half. Carol and I, and a few others, quickly decided that we'd cycle behind those girls who were enthusiastic about the idea of a race. The photographer was very late. He didn't appear until we were waiting for our taxis to travel home, so the photo session was rescheduled for the stage, before the show that night.

Next, we all went off to the carol service at All Saints'. There was a large congregation, and I couldn't help but wonder what had brought all these English-speaking people to Genoa at Christmas time. We girls were in very good voice. Not surprising, as we'd been singing carols in the dressing room since Torino.

Back at the theater right before the show, I picked up my mail. I'd received a lovely Christmas card from my brother and in big letters on the front was written, "Hurry Back." Then the photographer arrived. We'd dressed in our cycle race outfits and chignons, fully expecting he'd want us to pose in a line-up, but instead he wanted us to crouch near the ground, positioning ourselves to start a sprint running race, waiting for the starter's gun. This produced another explosion from Vera, and so there was no line-up, no "On your mark," and to settle the matter, Dapporto joined us on stage for some comedy photos.

During the show, as soon as midnight passed, everyone wished each other *"Auguri"* and *"Buon Natale."* Everyone gave each other air kisses so as not to mess up our stage make-up. The show had started a little earlier than usual, so we didn't have to wait until 1:30 a.m. for the company gift exchange, but it took place when we girls were getting changed after the show, when none of us were wearing make-up. This was probably the first time most members of the company had seen any of the girls without make-up, and as Sophie joked, "for many, this must've been a Christmas of disillusionment."

After the gift exchange, all the members of the company plus their visiting families went for a meal at a restaurant as the guests of Marisa del Frate, and arrived home at around 4 a.m. We then gave each other our personal presents. Annie gave me underclothes and a very pretty nightie and, from "The Bluebell Girls," I received a charm for my new bracelet, a *Cornicello*; the Italian lucky horn.

All evening I'd been on pins and needles because at 5 a.m. I was to receive a phone call from my boyfriend in Canada. All the girls were very excited for me and during the show, at the end of the Salvation Army Parade, (a scene in the first Act), Annie announced that none of "our set" (the girls who commonly congregated in our room) were to go to sleep early as they'd be needed to cheer me up after my phone call. Soon after 5 a.m. Jenny came to the door to say she could hear a phone ringing. It was behind a locked door. She and Sylvia battered on the door to no avail. There was an extension in the hall, but I'd already tried that, and it didn't appear to be connected to anything. Jenny found another phone in the hall and pulled and pushed every button in sight and finally got through. When I picked up the receiver and heard the operators talking to each other: "Is that New York?," "Is that Rome?" the adrenalin soared. Is there anything more exciting than being in the midst of such a transaction? But, that moment, hearing the operators, was the high point of the call. Ian and I had a short, impersonal exchange and beyond that we had absolutely nothing to say to each other. We hardly knew each other; we'd only had a few dates, and although we'd exchanged many, many letters (I reckon I'd written around 100,000 words between the previous summer and Christmas) that's not the same as face-to-face. I was self-conscious and shy, and the call was a total disappointment. At the time, after the call, I thought we should have planned the call, and had some conversation topics lined up, but in my twenty-one-year-old brain I didn't think that that's how romantic conversations were supposed to transpire.

Many of the other girls, picking up on the excitement created by my call, called home during the day. And having been on an international call once that day, now having some expertise, I did the same. So between the shows, I surprised my parents with a phone call. It was wonderful to hear them. When the operator got through to the house, Daddy picked up the receiver and as the operator said, "There's a call from Italy." Daddy screamed, "Italy!" His excitement was the best Christmas gift I could possibly have received. My brother had just left the house, but Daddy was able to catch him, so I spoke to Mummy, Daddy, my brother and grandma. My Canadian call may have been a disappointment, but the call to my family more than made up for it.

As already mentioned, we had two shows on Christmas Day. Some Christmas! I remember looking out at the audience and resenting the fact that I was working, and they were enjoying Christmas at my expense. And I wasn't alone. None of us were happy about it. However, one could argue that we were fortunate; when we were on stage we were surrounded by our friends, our whole community, so we weren't missing out on anything. But most members of the cast had their families visiting them, so when they were on stage, they were missing out on sharing their holiday.

Someone had been listening to our prayers and on December 27th, the day of the cycle race, it was raining. It was unfortunately rescheduled for the 29th. No one was looking forward to it, either the race or the dinner we were to attend afterwards, where we'd mingle with journalists, but the event had been much publicized so we couldn't get out of it.

Holiday season or not, Vera was as ever in a foul mood, telling us she was "wiping her hands of us" there and then. (We were thrilled. We wanted that more than anything, but we didn't think it would really happen.) She told us "there might as well not be a Captain for the amount of notice anyone took of her," and "I don't know why Miss Bluebell wastes her money having a Captain," and on and on. I was told that Miss Bluebell had given her a terribly small Christmas present in comparison to what she had normally received, and it seemed she was taking it as a hint that they wanted her to go. I felt sorry for her: she felt her age creeping up and she'd soon be out of a job. Although I knew that the Stardust had recently had a thirty-five-year-old Captain, that was not the norm, so Vera certainly had to be near her retirement.

We were told that Miss Bluebell would be coming to see us in San Remo, which I found myself looking forward to. We hadn't seen her since the first day in Milan and I preferred her to Mr. Libo. She was direct, with a no-nonsense approach to matters at hand. Mr. Libo was personable and very competent, but always seemed somewhat devious and made me feel uncomfortable, probably because of his somewhat unsavory reputation.

A day or so after Christmas I received a card in the mail notifying me that there was a parcel waiting at the Post Office. I knew it was a gift from Ian, so I raced out of the theater to order a taxi, and then reread the card and noticed that the pick-up time was between 10 a.m.-11:30 a.m. It was already too late in the day, so, disappointed, I had a late lunch with Carol. The next morning (the day of the bike race), at the appropriate time, I went to the Post Office. While I was waiting to be served, I watched customers go up to the counter and the official behind the desk opened the parcel, and took a long time over it; they inspected each Christmas gift and card. It was really frustrating to watch, to see a bureaucrat opening up people's gifts, while the rightful recipients stood there, helpless.

Eventually it was my turn. How dare this man usurp my moment of expectant joy, I fumed, as he unwrapped a gift that'd been sent to me, not him. Eventually, we both got to see the gift. It was a very pretty, delicate, gold filigree brooch and earring set, each piece in the shape of a maple leaf. Of course, I was not allowed to take possession of my gift, and instead I heard lots of Italian, of which I only understood one word: *"prohibita."* I was trying to pick up from the man's body language how this transaction was going, and how it would be resolved, and if I had any say in the resolution. As I didn't think he would physically remove me, I just stood there, and repeated over and over, *"peché prohibita?"*—what I thought meant "why prohibited?"—knowing I wouldn't understand his response. Eventually he figured that this transaction wasn't going anywhere, so decided to take me through the alleys and streets of Genoa to the Customs Office. At the Customs Office, again they only spoke Italian, so they just shook their heads at me. I was then taken back to the Post Office. On the way back we passed the Tourist Information Office so went in there and the man who was giving me the tour of Genoa explained the situation to the Tourist Officer who translated for me. He explained that one couldn't import anything into Italy, and that if I wanted to keep the gift, I would have to pay a 100% import duty. I said I was willing to do this, so the man from the Post Office said he'd write a letter on my behalf to the Customs Office, and I would be able to pay and have the goods.

We went back to the Post Office and the man's supervisor wrote the letter while I was taken into a back room where I was told to put the gift in my handbag and pay what I liked. I gave him a £1,000 note. "*Poco*," he frowned. I asked, "How many do you want?" He held up the fingers of one hand, so I gave him a £5,000 note. He pocketed the £1,000 and when his supervisor returned, he showed him the £5,000 note and they appeared to come to an understanding that they'd received an adequate amount. The jewelry was valued at £11,000.

In the afternoon, at the track, the photographers lined us up, one bike in each lane, and photographs were taken which later appeared in *Oggi* with the caption, "The most beautiful cyclists in the world." We posed, balanced on our bikes, with one hand on the handlebars and the other on our neighbor's shoulder. In the photo, I look nervous about losing my balance, my bike was very close to the neighbor whose shoulder I'm resting my hand on, leaving my other neighbor, Jessie, too far away to put her hand on my shoulder, and an unaesthetic gap in the line of cyclists.

We first cycled halfway around the track, looking beautiful, while the band from the show played the music from the show. This part I managed. We then started the race, and I reached the first corner still sitting on my bike. That was where my front wheel became entangled with Sophie's back wheel and my bike and I parted company, my face hitting the ground, my nose streaming with blood. People rushed to help me up, and as I turned around, there lying in the middle of the track was my chignon! Photographers rushed up to catch this unfortunate scene and I was helped off the field, one hand on my nose, and the other holding my tiny ponytail, hoping no one would notice that my chignon was missing!

Guido, my admirer from the vocal quartet, kindly helped me walk into the changing room—where he immediately attempted to kiss me! I wriggled free.

I've no idea who won the soccer match, and I vaguely remember that Sophie won the race. We were told we were going to sit with the journalists at the publicity dinner later that night, and we found the notion of keeping up a conversation, in Italian, throughout a meal, amusing, if not far-fetched. Anyway, our fears turned out to be baseless, as we ended up sitting in a separate area. This was the usual set-up at such events. We rarely mixed with regular folk because, so we understood, our "branding" was that we were more "up-market" than other chorus-girls and we should be looked upon and admired, not "chatted-up." It was hoped by those who employed us that if we were treated as though we were classy, then we would act as though we were classy.

Of course, the whole event was a bad idea. I heard that Vera was scared stiff that I was seriously hurt from the fall because the Director of the company had told her the previous night that he would take no responsibility if any of the girls were hurt. By the next day I developed an awful pain in my neck, back of my head, top of my back and arms, and in my waist on the side of my body where I fell. I thought I'd hit the track with only the side of the one leg, and my face, but maybe some of the other aches resulted from what I unknowingly, but instinctively, had done to protect myself. The next night I told Vera that I had millions of aches and pains, and she retorted, "Haven't we all!"

I was getting a reputation for being mishap prone. First there was the early-morning stuck-in-the-lift episode in Padua, and now I'd been sprawled on the track in Genoa. Members of the company would pass me backstage, smile, shake their heads, and mutter, "It could only happen to *Elizabetta*." The girls were more direct, accusing me of falling off my bike on purpose so that I didn't have to finish the race!

The show on New Year's Eve started a little earlier than normal, with a shorter intermission so that it would end before midnight. It was an invited audience, and they hardly applauded any of the scenes. After the show, we'd been invited to the front of the theater, so we went in search of what we imagined would be just the company having a drink. Instead, we found many of the invited audience already seated in the bar, which had been transformed by the addition of many tables, all set for a beautiful meal. Tons of champagne flowed, with guests sending many bottles to our table and there was a band and dancing. At 1 a.m.—midnight in

England—we begged for, and succeeded in getting, the band to repeat their performance of Auld Lang Syne. As was usual at such events, at first people just looked at us, but by 3:15 a.m. the ice was broken, and we were starting to mix with the rest of the guests and enjoy ourselves. That was when Vera told us that it was time we should leave as we had two shows the next day. It was a pity, as we so rarely mixed with people outside of the theater. But she was right, we all needed sleep.

I don't think I focused much on how I'd changed in the course of the tour so far, but I had. For one thing, I was happy. I'd become one of the group. I looked like a Bluebell, I felt like a Bluebell, I danced like a Bluebell—well, as far as the members of the audience were concerned, even if Vera might not have agreed. I enjoyed living with so many women, so it was hard to be lonely. It would've been nice to have a "best friend" as some of the girls had, but there was always company available. Although I was often not pleased with how Vera treated us, I had very few one-on-one altercations with her because I wasn't much trouble to her. I obeyed her rules. Now, my only rule infringement would be in the order of having a wisp of hair flying in the wind when I was on stage, a Bluebell "no, no."

And I liked the work. I enjoyed dancing and I found entertaining an audience every night a satisfying way to earn a living.

CHAPTER NINE

THE ITALIAN RIVIERA

The train journey from Genoa to San Remo was beautiful, running along the coast, with spectacular views of the Italian Riviera. The sky was blue and so was the water. At the time I thought the sea was reflecting the sky, but I now know that the Mediterranean Sea is blue because it doesn't have sufficient nutrients to support algae, resulting in taking on a vivid shade of blue; something I wanted my eyes to commit to memory.

The mountains went straight down to the Mediterranean so the train track would skirt around the mountains on a narrow ledge, across viaducts and through tunnels, many tunnels. Now and then we would pass a rocky beach where a hotel and an open-air swimming pool had been built, and other times we'd pass small communities where we'd see women with either baskets of flowers, or baskets of laundry, balanced on their heads.

In San Remo we checked into a lovely hotel up on a hill away from the beach. It was expensive, but our room had a private bathroom, a rare luxury, and dinner was included, to be served to us at 7 p.m. each night.

After dropping our suitcases and admiring our bathroom, we hurried down the hill to the theater, looking for mail. The theater was inside the Casino, a dramatic Art Nouveau building, which also housed a night club, gambling rooms and innumerable bars. I'd never seen anything like the town of San Remo: palm trees, rarely seen in England, were everywhere and there were also giant cacti, the size of trees. It was so exotic it looked like a movie set. I was told that it was the city where the wealthy Milanese came for the coldest months of winter and I could believe it.

After we checked for mail, we walked back to the hotel, and discovered the hill was very steep; it'd been so much easier when we'd arrived, riding in a taxi. We expected to have to return to the theater at 6 p.m. but were told the stage wasn't ready so we didn't have a rehearsal and, instead, had two hours to ourselves before the meal in the hotel dining room. Jessie called and implored me to continue my letter writing in her room, and having no good reason to turn her down, I went to her room, wrote a little, and chatted for the rest of the afternoon.

At 7 p.m. we went to the hotel restaurant for our dinner. That was when we discovered that we were to be offered a set menu. Vera went "up in the air" about this, and told the hotel management, in no uncertain terms, that we "weren't to be told what we were to eat," adding, "it's bad enough being told at what hour we were to eat." They wouldn't expand the menu, so she told us we were moving out, and that the following morning she would search for cheaper accommodation.

By 11:45 a.m. the next morning she'd found another hotel. The new hotel was only a little less expensive than the current one, but unfortunately all the *pensiones* she'd seen (usually considerably less expensive than hotels) were awful, so we were to move to another hotel. We had to be ready to leave by 1 p.m. At about 12:30 p.m. she was back. She'd told the hotel management we were leaving, and they claimed we owed them payment for the whole week. She told them that was impossible as we couldn't possibly afford it. So, the hotel reduced its price, but the price no longer included dinner, but now included breakfast. So, that's how we ended up; no richer, but we kept our private bathroom.

Meanwhile, on the day we arrived, some students, home from college for the winter holiday, had been in touch. They were friends of the old Bluebells, who knew them from previous appearances in San Remo. They asked if we'd go out with them that night. Angelo, the proprietor of a restaurant on the seafront, the Sud-Est, had invited us all for an after-hours meal. Five of us went, including Vera. The restaurant was closed to the public and the only guests were the students and the Bluebells. It was not an upscale restaurant but comfortable, and we were served a good meal, always the way to a Bluebell's heart (as I mentioned earlier). The ambiance was wonderful. There was an open fireplace, and we enjoyed the late night gathering with music, dancing, and conversation. And even better, between songs, we could hear the sound of waves outside. And for the first time on the tour, a young man paid attention to me, and what's more, I didn't discourage him.

You might wonder why I felt that this was the first young man to pay attention to me. What about Guido, the member of the vocal quartet, who'd certainly paid attention to me? A brief explanation: Guido was definitely attractive but definitely married and, if that weren't enough, had an ongoing relationship with Carol. Next, I was very suspicious of his motivations. Firstly, I reckoned he saw me as a "back-up" to his on-going relationship with Carol, and secondly, I had the sneaking suspicion that his Italian ego would be stoked if he managed to seduce the one Bluebell who appeared, through her constant letter-writing and her lack of liaisons with members of the company, to be incredibly loyal to a boyfriend in Canada. What a "feather in his cap" that would be! So, there were plenty of reasons to discount the attention he paid me.

So, when it came to someone new paying attention to me, I was aware that the chief attraction was that I was a Bluebell Girl, but that was fine with me. The next day the girls told me more about my admirer, Paulo. He'd been engaged to one of the Bluebells in the show the year before. She just happened to be a girl that I'd previously heard about, because, it seemed, I looked somewhat like her. The next time I saw him I asked about the relationship. It seemed a very reasonable question. He just scowled and said she "was not a nice girl." I understood that to mean that he was man who'd been rejected.

During our time in San Remo, members of the company gambled at the Casino and, so we understood, were winning. When we left the theater at 2 a.m. each morning it was extraordinary to see patrons entering the building. In other cities, when we left the theater each night, the world outside was in total blackness, with no humans in sight. Those of us who were over twenty-one were offered a free pass to enter the gambling rooms at any time, but Vera told us that she didn't think we should gamble. I wasn't planning on it and didn't. That was the first time I'd ever seen a gambling casino. I was amazed there were so many elderly gamblers. All the old people I'd ever known held on to their money!

I saw Paulo several times that week. He was not a student, but an officer on a Texaco oil tanker, staying at home while he studied for a promotional examination. We took walks near the water and harbor before and after the show and, depending on the time of day, enjoyed a meal or hot chocolate. I wasn't terribly enamored, but he was definitely more interesting than the men in the company as he was more sophisticated, his English was good, and I definitely liked the attention. Plus, I was seeing more of San Remo than any of the other towns we'd visited, where I usually saw only the hotel and theater. Needless to say, he was hoping for more than a passing friendship. This suddenly became clear to me when, late one night after the show, we were walking amongst the yachts docked in the harbor, and it suddenly dawned on me that Paulo and I were about to be alone on one of those luxurious boats. A figurative flare went up, telling me I was losing control of the situation; I quickly announced it was time to return to the hotel and the moment passed. In addition to this, mostly pleasant, complication in my life, Guido of the vocal quartet was still pursuing me. He must've recently fallen out with Carol, so he needed company.

January 6th was Epiphany, a holiday, so we had the afternoon free. The 5 *Brutos*, who we knew from Milan, were performing in the Casino's Night Club in the afternoon, so we called in to see them. When we arrived, people were dancing, and Bruno Martins and his band were playing one of "our" show's tunes. The 5 *Brutos* were performing at a children's party in the Big Room in the Casino (Epiphany is a festival for the children), so off we went to the party, where we were amazed by the display of wealth, both the adults and children arriving in fur coats! It was the first time we had seen the 5 *Brutos* perform their slapstick act, which reminded me of the Three Stooges.

On our final night, the students threw us a farewell party at the Sud-Est. We had only one show and it began early, so we were out of the theater at 8 p.m. This was my first experience of an Italian gathering where only personal friends had been invited, and I enjoyed it far more than any English party I'd attended. In Birmingham and London, at the only parties I'd experienced, a number of guests, usually the same ones each time, would drink too much, and this was the accepted sign of a successful party. San Remo was different. No one drank too much, which to an almost non-drinker like me, was very comforting. Everyone remained charming and friendly, and everyone had a good time. If this was typical, the English could learn from the Italians. Something else the English could learn from the Italians: the party included an excellent meal. We then took a last walk around the yacht harbor and ended up at the Whisky A Go Go, a local club, where we bumped into the 5 *Brutos*, in the audience this time, and also Deanna with Delio.

The next morning, we left San Remo. Train-call was at 7:45 a.m., an incredibly early hour for us; we hardly knew that such an hour existed! We were all sad to be leaving, but after only about three hours of sleep we were on our way to Livorno, which I'd been warned was awful, but we were to be there for only two days, and then on to Rome, moving south at last. We also received some items of news: first, Enzo would return to the show in Livorno and, second, Miss Bluebell, who never did arrive in San Remo, might be visiting us in Rome.

For once, Dapporto was traveling on the train rather than in his car. He came to chat with us in our compartment and described his experiences when touring with his show during World War II. He told us that the company would arrive in a city and find that the theater had been bombed the previous night. This had been the case in December 1942 when they were to appear at the Alfieri in Torino, the theater where we'd recently appeared. The facade—built in 1855—was the only piece still standing.

Our train journey took us back along the Italian Riviera and, as the previous week, the journey was beautiful and the Italian coastline, stunning. There was hardly a cloud in the sky, and as I looked through the window of the train the sun was shining onto my face. Growing up in England, sun shining on my face was always a novelty.

I was sitting there surrounded by sleeping girls, some of them having had even less sleep than me the previous night. I was tired. This had been the first town that I was not eager to leave. Yes, part of that was due to an admirer paying attention to me, but San Remo and its environs were gorgeous in January 1961, particularly if you had grown up in post-war Birmingham!

CHAPTER TEN

ROMA

We were in Rome at last. Of course, our first mission upon arrival was to check out the *pensione*, our home for the next five weeks. It was near the theater and we were sleeping two to a room, and the rooms were quite acceptable. All good news! The building boasted a rather rickety lift, and it had a sign *"Attenzione,"* which we faithfully obeyed. Per the sign: ascending, it took three passengers, descending, only two. I always imagined a crowd of people stranded at the top.

Next morning our large suitcases arrived from Genoa and, incidentally, it was another day with no work. After unpacking we all went shopping to stock up on cotton wool, hairpins, hairnets, and all the other necessities of our working lives, and I went further afield looking for long leather gloves to replace those I'd lost at the bicycle race in Genoa. This was an easy purchase as Italy was known for its abundant and reasonably priced leather goods. It was exciting to be in a big, bustling city once again. It reminded me of being in London, and I was thrilled to be passing historic sites, such as the Spanish Steps and the Fountain of Trevi, both within blocks of the *pensione.*

That evening we relaxed. Alice was in our room, gluing picture postcards in her Bluebell scrapbook, while the three of us debated the advisability of throwing coins in the Fountain of Trevi (Annie and Alice's love lives weren't going well so they weren't sure they wanted to return to Rome.)

About this time, we were hungry and wanted a snack, which would involve leaving the *pensione* and visiting a store. We saw a problem! Upon our arrival in Rome, Vera had given us special "Now we're in Rome" instructions: when we ventured outside the *pensione* or theater we must *always* look respectable. (I'm not sure how this differed from her standard rules to live by.) Unfortunately, Annie was already in her baby-doll pajamas with rollers in her hair and I was already undressed, so there was no way we were going to take the time and effort needed to look our best. Annie took out her rollers and, with Annie in her pajamas, me in my underclothes and sweater, we put on our overcoats, and headed out. By Bluebell standards, this was incredibly daring. Vera would have been fit to be tied if we'd been hit by a bus and she'd found us in a hospital in anything less than our best. We crossed the road very carefully.

Because we had the important Rome Opening the following evening, we'd been told to be in our rooms by 10 p.m. that evening and, surprise, surprise, the only one who wasn't home was Vera. It gradually dawned on us what was up. Of course! Giorgio lived in Rome! We had naïvely assumed that as his wife also lived in Rome that he wouldn't be spending time with Vera. We were so naïve. Giorgio wouldn't let a little thing like a wife interfere with his love life.

The afternoon of the opening, we had a rehearsal. Franco Pisano, the composer of the show's music, was also in the theater, listening to the orchestra rehearse. He hadn't heard his music since Milan, and he was disappointed. It seems there was a difference of musical interpretation between him and our Orchestra Director, Pasquale Frustaci. The latter had had an illustrious career composing pop music—the Glenn Miller Army Air Force Band had recorded his song "*Tu, solamente tu*" ("You, Fascinating You")—and maybe he enjoyed adding his take on Franco's music. Maybe he had to be reminded that it's the composer's intention that counts.

Now to be honest, the orchestra sounded completely different to us also; different because it was a fuller sound. Since Milan, we'd been traveling with a reduced orchestra—only a pianist, percussion, brass and wind—but now, in Rome, strings had been added back. I liked the sound but understood that we'd only be hearing it in Rome. When we started touring again, we'd be hearing the reduced sound once more.

The dancers didn't associate with members of the orchestra, other than the pianist and percussionist who we'd shared the stage with during rehearsals, and even that relationship was greatly reduced once the show opened. There was only one occasion during the tour when we gave them any thought; that was the night that Vera and Maestro Frustaci, "had words." Vera had given him a "ticking-off" for some now-long-forgotten musical-directing error—possibly beginning the music for a number before we were fully ready on stage or taking a number a little too fast. In doing so she had given no thought to the fact that our fate on stage was largely in his musical hands. The next time we performed the Salvation Army number—a pseudo-military along-the-lines-of a Rockettes number—he chose to remind her of his power: he played the music just a tad slower than we were used to. We were on stage before we realized what was happening, so we couldn't discuss this curveball being thrown at us, we just had to wing it. We held it together, but it was very disconcerting. Being forced to move to slower music meant we had to take the exact same size steps, but take longer over each one, your foot hovering for a millisecond in mid-air. In this particular number the choreography required that we precision-march in wheel formations, then break into smaller formations, and so on, ending up in a line at the front of the stage. Vera never complained to Maestro Frustaci again.

Our rehearsal ended. We assumed that the composer and the Orchestra Director had a meeting of the minds, and the hour of the Opening arrived. The auditorium was beautiful, with flowers hanging from both the *passerella* and the boxes close to the stage. We wanted the show to be a success in Rome, and we needed good press reviews, so we gave our best performance. Yes, we always gave our best performance, but it was still possible to give it a little more, so we did.

The costumes had been cleaned (the only time they were cleaned during the tour) and some had shrunk. Our costumes were tight to begin with so there wasn't much room for shrinkage. Jenny, who was wearing Christine's costumes (who was thinner than Jenny), had to have her Finale Act I costume extended. The zip just wouldn't meet, so the dresser threaded elastic across the back to hold it together.

The next day we were eager to see what the press had to say, so we attempted to read a review of the show. We didn't understand much of it, but it said something about the Blue-bells being "sophisticated" but "rather impersonal," and then something about the costumes which we didn't understand. (Maybe the reviewer noticed they were clean, but a bit tight!) The best news was that, overall, the reviewer liked the show. We were happy; we liked full houses!

The next day, I ached. The result of having two days with no exercise (a travel day and then a rest day) and then a day with both a rehearsal and a show.

Soon after the opening, Miss Bluebell arrived in Rome. She was wearing a gorgeous outfit and looked very attrac-tive. After watching the show, she told us we were a good troupe and were working hard. (No one ever thought to, pub-licly, give Vera credit for our being a good troupe. Hopefully Miss Bluebell did in private.) She had criticisms for a few of the girls but said nothing to me although I heard, probably from Vera, that she liked the color of my hair; that it made me "look brighter." Regardless, I wasn't nervous as I didn't need another job. I'd come to the conclusion that, although I wasn't the world's best dancer, I'd no particular negatives, such as peculiar or adverse mannerisms on stage. Some of the newer Bluebells did. They looked into the flies when they danced, others onto the floor, and still others tended to dis-tort their faces into odd expressions.

We learned that twelve more Bluebells, many coming di-rectly from the Lido, would be arriving shortly in Rome for a twelve-week television contract, and either Miss Bluebell or Mr. Libo would be in Rome throughout the twelve-week period, so we could look forward to them popping in and out of the theater throughout our Rome run.

A few nights later we received more compliments. The producers of the shows at the Lido and the Stardust, who both happened to be in Rome, saw the show. They liked what they saw and reported back to Miss Bluebell that we were a good troupe. Last year, when they were back in Paris after seeing the show, they had reported that some of the girls were "not up to it," but this year they seemed satisfied.

There was more good news. The show would be going to Venice after all: we'd be appearing at the Casino on the Lido in Venice during Easter Week. I briefly wondered how the scenery was going to navigate the canals and low bridges but had to assume that someone had figured that out.

We were enjoying enthusiastic audiences in Rome. Imagine our delight when, one night, we spied King Farouk (the former King of Egypt) in the audience. He was in the center of the orchestra section, with a very messy-haired girlfriend. He was wearing regular glasses, not the dark sunglasses he was known for, and he applauded and smiled a lot. We'd been seeing photographs of him in the English tabloids for so many years, and he appeared so much more pleasant in the flesh, maybe because he was enjoying the show so much.

Near the end of January, we were all invited to a party. We were picked up after the show in a couple of cars. One was driven by the fiancé of Ricki, a friend of Kate's, and the other by an American, a pilot. We drove across Rome on a brightly lit autostrade, past the Nervi-engineered Palazzetto dello Sport and the Olympic Village, which had been built for the 1960 Olympics. We then transferred to a road that climbed steeply to an area where, high on a hill, two apartment buildings stood. We were led to the penthouse apartment of one of the buildings. It was gorgeous. Standing inside it was like standing inside an *Architectural Digest* photo spread. Once we'd all made it into the entrance hall, taken a quick look at our surroundings and the people gathered there, we turned to each other and mouthed, in unison, *La Dolce Vita*, referring to the recently released Fellini movie. (The one which depicted the decadent social life that currently existed around Via Veneto, in Rome.)

The apartment was a huge glass box. It had an incredibly high ceiling with at least two walls of glass that overlooked the lights of Rome, a dramatic freestanding fireplace and chimney, and a freestanding staircase that wound up into the heavens. Quite amazing, especially for a girl who six-months earlier had been living in a London bed-sitter.

The party was pleasant and definitely not *La Dolce Vita*. First, we were served a meal, which was followed by dancing and conversation. I found myself seated next to a Ferrari race-driver who only spoke Italian, but I managed to keep up a "conversation" for several hours in my grammarless Italian. With my stunted vocabulary I can't think what I talked about. Even so, he called the next day, wanting to see me again. I gave him the usual Bluebell line, that a "friend" was "arriving from Milan."

We'd been told that our host was Ricki's boyfriend, but heard later that that story had been concocted to discourage the paparazzi. On arriving at the party, we discovered that our host was a well-known actor named Antonio (I never did catch his last name). He was tall, dark, and tanned. Monica, who fancied herself as the second Brigitte Bardot, (much to Vera's despair), made a beeline for him and succeeded in winning what she saw as the evening's first prize: when we left, she remained at the flat.

In our other life, backstage at the theater, we were all fond of the dancers' chief dresser, Annette; a middle-aged Italian woman who traveled with us from town to town, making our work lives easier. We were responsible for getting ourselves ready for each number, but she was the one, along with her helpers, who was there to support us. Her endless good nature, constant hard work and problem-solving skills were a godsend. Anytime she sounded (she only spoke Italian) as though she was getting close to exasperation because a girl had misused her costume, we figured she was probably on the verge of swearing so we'd playfully threaten to tell "*il Papa*," (particularly now that we were in Rome, where the Vatican was so handy) then we'd all crumble into laughter. It was hard for her to stay mad!

I was always looking for diversions to make the repetitive nature of the work more interesting. In the *Orientale* number I didn't have to look very far—it was a beautiful dance with an ethereal aura about it and it was important that we maintain Mona Lisa smiles with, as mentioned earlier, no teeth in sight. However, I had a friendly elf standing in the wings whose one goal each night was to make me laugh! All the girls were fond of this elf. He was one of the show's resident backstage workers whom we nicknamed Noddy, after the Vera Blyton children's book character. He was always good humored, never tried to make physical contact with us, altogether unthreatening and, needless to say, very short. He was probably in his mid-forties, around five-feet tall, bald, and adorable.

We performed the *Orientale* in two lines, and I was at the end of the back line, right next to the wings, which was nice because if I messed up it was never noticeable to the audience. Noddy stood in the wings, hidden from the audience, but about three feet away from me, and danced the whole dance alongside me. He had the exotic hand movements down pat, he had the sweet Mona Lisa smile on his face, he stamped his feet when we stamped ours. You had to admire the man! Every night I had to struggle to hold back the laughter and maintain the Mona Lisa look.

But Noddy didn't stand in the wings alone. At the end of the dance there was a noisy finale. Lots of percussion, bells chiming, and us stamping our bare feet as we danced eight slow turns: Count "and," face the back; Count "one," face the audience; Count "and," face the back, and so on until we landed on eight, facing the audience, when the applause would ring through the theater.

This was tricky for a girl who one year earlier was a beginner dancer! So, I would count out loud, in English, ventriloquist-style, behind my Mona Lisa smile. After a few months of the show, with great concentration, I could count in silence, focusing intently on my silent counts. But I was thwarted by one of the electricians, Augusto, who figured out exactly what I was doing, and how he could help me out. He stood next to Noddy, a few feet from me, calling out any numbers that came into his head, "*due, nove, dieci, uno, tredici.*" So, I then had three things to focus on: blocking out Augusto's smiling presence in the wings, the proper count, and avoiding laughter!

Two groups evolved within the troupe: my "bedroom" set, consisting of Annie, Alice, Sophie, and Jessie, and my "dressing room bench" set, which was the four of us who shared the bench furthest from Vera—Sylvia, me, Jenny, and Kate. Sylvia, Jenny, and Kate were not intimidated by authority, so I loved being seated with them. None of us were expecting to remain with the Bluebell Girls following the current contract, and that gave everyone a little independence. Vera had little affection for us.

One night, a Sunday, when Vera was unwell and not dancing all the numbers, she sat in the audience, and between the shows she decided to critique the four of us. She took us each on in turn. First Kate and Jenny, then it was Sylvia's turn. Vera didn't like Sylvia's smile in the *Orientale.* "I want you to change your Mona Lisa smile. Copy Deanna's smile."

"No," retorted Sylvia. "I was chosen for the solo part because of my expression. Plus, Miss Bluebell, when she was here just three weeks ago, congratulated me on the way I danced the number."

And the final word from Vera, "I'm contacting Miss Bluebell. And I don't *ever* want you in my troupe again!"

Next, she started on me, "Whatever you happen to be doing after the contract and wherever you're going doesn't change the fact that you are earning your living here, and therefore you've got to get with it as far as your dancing is concerned." Not finished with me, she took a breath and spat out, "I'd expected *some* improvement in all of this time."

I can only think that sitting with Kate, Sylvia, and Jenny every night had given me some nerve! I heard myself saying, "For that very reason, I've always done my best. I've always known that if you thought I was slacking you could accuse me of not working because I didn't want another Bluebell contract."

She wouldn't let it drop, and continued in the same vein, on and on, and I responded by echoing what I'd already said. Then the final word, which came from me, "Anyway, Miss Bluebell doesn't have any complaints." She didn't answer, just walked off, mumbling that none of us on our bench liked being criticized.

Jenny had previously told me that Vera had told her, (back in Genoa), she couldn't "stand girls like Elizabeth who come into Bluebells just as though it were another job." Being a Bluebell should be a calling, apparently.

One evening Jenny told the three of us, in great secrecy, that she was going to marry her boyfriend, Coky, at the end of the contract. He had been a member of an acrobat act at the Stardust, the show that she'd just left. She didn't want Vera to find out, so she had to make sure that none of the other girls found out about it. She first had to write to her mother to let her know, but as she was only nineteen, she needed her parents' permission for marriage. For the rest of the evening, we made unhelpful suggestions as to what should be included in the letter. She thought her letter should be "telling" her mother the news, but we piped up, "But shouldn't you be asking her?"—which is not what she wanted to hear. On top of this, she was depressed. Not only had Coky (who'd been staying in Rome) traveled to Paris the previous night, but now that he'd left Rome, she had to return to our *pensione*, a definite downgrade from the accommodation she'd been sharing with Coky.

Good news came quickly from Jenny's mother, in the form of a "Best Wishes" telegram. Now that her parents had given her their blessing, Jenny wanted to leave the contract. She told us that when she had replaced Christine, she was told that if she didn't like the Dapporto tour she could leave, and now that the marriage was on, she said she felt restless and wanted to go.

I often chatted to Sylvia for hours. In fact, as a result, my accent became more clipped, and it lost some of its Midland sound. She would tell me about her family. She'd had a letter from her mother, where she told of attending a party where the Queen Mother and Princess Margaret were also guests. She'd written, "The Queen Mother was as charming as ever, and I'll leave my opinion of Margaret until you get home." Poor Princess Margaret, she was always in trouble.

Sylvia would teach me some social skills I hadn't needed previously, such as how to order from a menu or discuss my food preferences with a waiter. I was very self-conscious about such things as prior to coming to Italy I'd dined in an upscale restaurant only once in my life.

Sylvia and I would complain to each other that our brains were becoming sluggish, living as we were within the confines of Bluebell-dom, where the topics of conversation were so limited. We complained to each other that no one ever wondered "how" or "why" about anything or showed any curiosity regarding the outside world. I was just as guilty as anyone, though. I never purchased a copy of the *New York Herald*—what, use some of my savings?—and only went to the English language library in Rome once while we were there, and quickly became bored.

Instead, the four of us, Kate, Jenny, Sylvia, and I, formed a loosely organized anti-Vera fraternity. We called ourselves the "Senate" (seeing as we were in Rome) and my *nom-de-Rome* was Cassius (that is "Cassius," not "Gaius Cassius" of Julius Cesar fame). At the time we thought we were very entertaining and, if nothing else, it proved to be a diversion for all the girls, as we all had to deal with the stress that Vera caused. For example, when a girl was ill she'd receive little or no sympathy from Vera, but a girl could always rely on some warmth and understanding from us.

During the five weeks in Rome, we gave roughly forty performances. We all wanted the audience to see a perfect performance every time but, of course, that isn't what happened. One night there was no blue tinsel curtain to stand behind (or telephones) in the Presentation number; they must've all got stuck in the flies. Another night we danced the early part of the Hyde Park number in front of a backdrop from the prior scene, the Prince's bedroom, meanwhile stagehands were carrying off a wall and window!

Other memorable moments were the result of I know not what but, as the Bluebells would often say, "*Che divertimento.*" One night the show started at least fifteen minutes late. This was of great concern to the show's management because the stagehands wouldn't work beyond a certain hour. To resolve the problem the dialogue sections were shortened. My guess is that Dapporto, a comedian, was told to cut out the ad-libbing he did other nights. The result for the dancers, both boys and girls, was that the time between our numbers, the musical numbers, was shortened, but we had no advanced knowledge of by how much. We would suddenly hear our musical cues over the loudspeaker in the dressing room. The result was that we'd arrive in the wings still pulling long gloves up arms, or short gloves on wrong hands or, on occasion, making a late stage entrance.

Other times it was a dancer's health that got in the way. Kate missed several shows because she had a "bad stomach." Vera was mad with her, but Kate refused to do the show, saying she was too ill. Being an "old" Bluebell had its perks. I wonder if any of us new girls would've had the nerve to refuse to go on stage. The doctor was called; he diagnosed a liver problem.

Another night Annie returned to the *pensione* doubled up in pain even though Vera had given her painkillers at the theater. The lights went off early, at 3:30 a.m., but she woke me at 6:45 a.m., asking me to fetch Vera, who dosed her with more painkillers and Annie went back to sleep. The following day she was still in pain, but less so than the previous night. The doctor was called; again, the problem was the liver.

These weren't the only occasions that the visiting doctor identified the liver to be the cause of a dancer's pain. It appeared to be the Italians' catch-all diagnosis.

As expected, when the twelve Bluebells arrived in Rome for the eight-week TV contract, Mr. Libo watched every performance of our show. The challenge for each of us each evening was to find him in the audience, or flies, or whichever spot he'd selected to place his rotund body. He shared with us that the Director of the show had been very complimentary, saying we were so much better than the previous year's troupe, worked harder, and were better educated and better behaved. I've no idea what this meant; no one got drunk at the restaurants and we had several girls who spoke fluent Italian?

I was still saving to go to Canada. As most of our money went towards food, the easy way to save money was to eliminate one meal a day. Meals cost the equivalent of around nine shillings in a *trattoria* and sixteen shillings in a restaurant. This soon ate (pardon the pun) through the girls' salary. Put another way, if I ate at a restaurant twice a day, each week I'd be spending the equivalent of my total London take-home pay on meals. That irked me, so I tried to eat only one meal a day (apart from breakfast) and often ate that meal in a *trattoria*, rather than a restaurant, and have a hot chocolate if I felt peckish. I lost weight but didn't waste away. My tummy got flat, and my buttocks got smaller, neither of which I minded. Kate commented later in the contract that when I had joined the Bluebells, I had been a "tub."

One day it was announced that Mr. Libo was going back to Paris and wanted to know which girls wanted another contract. He came to the dressing room and asked each girl, in turn, what their plans were. As the other girls responded, I blanked out my mind and heard nothing; I didn't want my turn to answer to come around. I knew I was going to say "no", but I didn't want to hear myself announce to the world that I wouldn't dance again. That in a few weeks this would all come to an end; even though I knew, long-term, that is what I wanted, I was torn. I was regretting the fact that I was leaving the Bluebells. It was a wonderful way to see the world, and we all had such pride in being Bluebells. I felt special, and I didn't like the idea of losing that uniqueness. Nevertheless, when my turn came, I said, "no."

I wasn't the only one leaving. During the prior five months several girls said they wanted to leave at the end of the contract, but in the end, on that day, only two of us said we didn't want another job. Deanna was the other. She was a bit hesitant like me, not wanting to make the final break. She'd been with the Bluebells for three years and was leaving to stay with Delio. She didn't explain this at the time, but both Vera and Miss Bluebell were aware of it.

One afternoon I was in Monica's room and she was telling me that she was going to buy a dog that afternoon. I couldn't believe it! I tried desperately to dissuade her, telling her how it wouldn't be fair to the dog, living in hotels and trains. She assured me that she'd take it for walks often. I then put forward what I considered to be my trump card, that she'd have to buy a ticket for it when we traveled by train. I succeeded in making her stop and think, but who knows how deep her "stop and think" was. I could just see Vera's face if Monica rolled up to train-call with a dog!

Another afternoon Sophie shared with us her escapades on the stage at the Lido. She would have us rolling on our beds in laughter. She was only fifteen when she joined the Lido, and just as adorable as she still was. She would tell us of the many times she was in a kicking line and would kick in the wrong direction from the rest of the dancers; she would enter the stage late and rush straight across the stage, through the other dancers, to her place in line; and on one occasion, when she was the replacement soloist, standing alone on the top of some stairs that moved forward towards the audience, she walked down the stairs, was lifted by one of the boys, forgot what to do next so did an arabesque, and stepped straight into a curtain. She was a stunning, bright young woman; an utter delight, except to Vera, to whom she was a constant irritant, with her unkempt shoes and hose, and her complete lack of fear of authority.

The Captain of the Rome TV Bluebells was visiting us in our dressing room one evening, chatting to Jenny, who she'd worked with in Las Vegas. Jenny learned that when Vera heard about Jenny and Coky's Stardust relationship, she had told Miss Bluebell that Molly, Captain of the Las Vegas troupe, had been allowing the girls to have relationships with members of the company. Molly, who was by then the Captain at the Lido in Paris, got in lots of trouble with Miss Bluebell for this transgression. This was pretty mean of Vera but, on the other hand, it must've been galling to know that other Captains were ignoring the rule when she took such pains, and got such grief, in her attempts to enforce it!

It was about now that I had noticed a change in the girls' attitude to the two-show regime of our Sundays. In Milan, I would hear them say they were, "just in the mood to do two shows." Now they tended to agree with me, that it was horrible. Luckily for the audience our mood wasn't reflected in the quality of our performance. We were professionals through and through; the groaning went on in our hotel rooms, not on stage. And Sunday audiences tended to be receptive; they were relaxed, they hadn't been to work that day. But that didn't change the fact that throughout the first show it was awful doing a number knowing that you had to do it once again that day. The most wonderful moment was putting on the *Finalissimo* costume for the second time, and of course, it was even better when you were taking it off!

A week or two into the Rome run I received a letter from my mother. She was thinking of visiting me at Easter and wanted to know where we'd be at that time. As no dates were definite on the tour, I figured it would be best that she come to Rome for a few days. Not only was I certain of the Rome dates, but the city of Rome is unique! Every time you turned a corner you were seeing a never-to-be-forgotten sight. My mother, the "queen of the slideshow," would be in her element!

As she'd be traveling alone, it made sense that she should come by plane. She'd never traveled outside of England, didn't speak French or Italian and, although extremely agile, had an artificial leg (amputated when she was toddler, in the days before penicillin). The thought of her changing train stations in Paris and taking the overnight train to Rome was unthinkable. Flying to Rome was the solution. However, she'd always vowed she'd never, ever fly. This wasn't an uncommon sentiment at that time; commercial plane crashes were more common than in the twenty-first century. I went into persuasive daughter mode and wrote her a very heartfelt, eight-page letter. It turned out to be unnecessary: I soon received a response—actually two, in one envelope. One letter ended mid-sentence. The second, written a couple of days later, explained that in the middle of the first letter she had decided she'd go straight into Birmingham, had bought her plane ticket—which I'd be paying for with money I owed her—and was now in the throes of getting a passport.

We had a rehearsal on the afternoon my mother was to arrive, so I was late at the Air Terminal in downtown Rome. Fortunately, she arrived an hour later than expected after enduring an arduous day for a neophyte international traveller.

That morning she'd flown from Birmingham to Heathrow and, upon arriving at Heathrow, found that she was the only Rome passenger not notified that the flight was to leave from Gatwick Airport. The airline put her in a car and ferried her across London where she was put on a later plane, one where she was the only passenger except for a group of men sitting at the front and, when it stopped in Rome to refuel she was let off, the only person on the plane to do so!

She had been absolutely thrilled by the flight and her first close-up views of clouds and spectacular alpine mountaintops as she crossed Switzerland and northern Italy.

This was the first time I'd seen anyone from my pre-Bluebell days. She didn't recognize me until I waved. I liked that. All the hard work had been worth it—or was it just that I was blonde and a bit thinner? It was wonderful to see her. We had dinner, and later she watched the show, which of course she thought was wonderful. (Maybe it was a better show if you didn't understand a word of the dialogue.) And we talked and talked until we were both hoarse and I caught up on all the news from home. She'd brought with her a twenty-first birthday gift from an aunt, a beautiful ring, as well as chocolates and a box of All-Bran.

She wasn't happy when she found out that I didn't eat after the show and said that wasn't going to happen while she was in Rome, but after a stressful travel day, she changed her mind. Instead, after the show, before we went to bed at 2:45 a.m., we walked to the Fountain of Trevi. The water wasn't flowing as it was the middle of the night, but it was floodlit and so beautiful; I couldn't have planned a better "welcome to Rome."

She stayed with me for four full days, and she proved herself a real trouper! She watched the show every night except one, and on that night, she sat in the dressing room. And every day we took at least one Cook's Bus Tour, seeing the sights of Rome. We both had very little sleep. We'd have the lights off at 2:30 a.m. and be up at 8 a.m. and be off to see the Catacombs, the Holy Steps, Villa Borghese, the Sistene Chapel, St. Peter's Basilica, the Pantheon, and more. Had my mother not visited I would have seen very little of this wonderful city.

One of the days my mother was with me, February 14, was a Gala Day, *Martedi Grasso* (Fat Tuesday). Seven of the girls decided to go to an artists' club and they insisted my mother and I join them. When we arrived at the club, we found the place in true, raucous, gala mode. Our entrance was announced over the loudspeakers, and we walked in to loud applause, so my mother got to experience how it felt to be a Bluebell. The show was wonderful too, featuring some amazing dancers from a local African-American strip show.

All too soon my mother left for home and I immediately missed her company. Annie had moved to Deanna's room while my mother was with me, and hadn't moved back, so I'd wake up to an empty room, which I hadn't done for months. I was fine, though; we were ending our stay in Rome and I was busy organizing my suitcases, ready to be sent ahead to Florence, where we'd be arriving in a week's time.

CHAPTER ELEVEN

STELLA ARRIVES, JENNY LEAVES

From Rome we headed north to Perugia, a beautiful medieval city located on a hill half-way between Rome and Florence, known for its many universities and the Perugina *Baci*, the ubiquitous "chocolate kiss" candy. On the train Monica had to suffer some teasing due to a recent conquest. At the artists' club we'd visited a few nights earlier, she'd met an actor who told her he'd played Jesus Christ in the movie *Ben Hur*, and during the past few days she'd seen a lot of him. We were unmerciful, saying "Surely Jesus Christ must be your greatest conquest." She countered she was "not in the *moot*" to be teased.

The good news was that Monica did not arrive at the train-call with a dog. Had she done so it would have caused obvious complications, even if the dog would have been enjoyed by all. There were quite a few dogs passing in and out of the company. Marisa had a lovely little mongrel called "Cinders," a high-energy dog whom everyone adored; he was often the only cheerful one at train-call. There was also a wire-haired terrier that visited now and then when he was brought by the wife of an elderly actor in the show, and also there had been a puppy acquired by the actress, Wilma, in San Remo that, come to think of it, we hadn't seen since. And lastly, a puppy that Franco had bought in Genoa. He took the pup in his car to see his family at Christmas in Torino, but on the way wrecked his car in the snow. With no car he had to travel back to Genoa by train, and at the station discovered that he needed a ticket for the dog. Not only that, he found that the ticket cost more than his own ticket. So, he turned to his parents who were there to see him off, handed them the dog, and left.

We performed two shows in Perugia. The theater was large, no complaints about this, but the *passerella* was incredibly long, which meant that we had the challenge of racing along the *passerella* while not plowing into the girl ahead, which could happen when facing the audience and barely looking where we were going.

Around this time Vera decided that I would look better if I wore false eyelashes on stage. Some girls wore them, others didn't. It depended on whether Vera thought they improved your look. Whenever Vera had brought up the subject previously, I'd always avoided agreeing to wear them. I didn't want to make the purchase out of my precious savings but more importantly, I didn't want to add another task to the already lengthy endeavor of applying stage make-up. Anyway, I pulled a face and she let the matter drop—but I didn't know for how long.

The next day we woke at 11 a.m., caught a train around 1 p.m., slept our way to Florence, and performed a show that night. Once agan, we were performing in a theater with an Italian style auditorium, with its many tiers of boxes, and once again there was a *passerella* issue. This time it took a long time to get from the main area of the stage to the *passerella* and, having reached the *passerella*, it again was incredibly long. And, of course, still only the same number of available measures of music!

The audience was enthusiastic. Dapporto told us that live shows are appreciated in Florence because many of the old aristocracy lived there and they were "still of the old school who appreciate live entertainment." He added that Florence was in Tuscany and that the *Tuscani* were the "true" Italians. And, to validate the good reception, the next day we received an excellent review in the local newspaper.

Following Vera's eyelash comments, I gathered that she expected me to do something about my appearance on stage, so I decided to improve my stage make-up. I added shading to accentuate my cheek bones, dabbed a light color beneath the re-drawn lifted arch of my eyebrows, and dots (lipstick applied with an orange stick), at the inside edge of my eyes. The changes made me look more glamorous (so I thought), accentuating my facial bone structure. This must've satisfied Vera because she never again pressured me to add false eyelashes to my "look."

The next day Vera and Jessie had to rush to the British Consulate. According to her out-of-date paperwork, Jessie wasn't officially in Italy any longer, and her passport was set to expire in two days. On the way there they bumped into a very affectionate Kate and Luciano. Poor Vera—she must've felt that this flagrant display of Bluebell-rule-breaking, which followed the now very public relationship between Deanna and Delio, was a direct challenge to her authority. It now was obvious to Vera that Kate had been lying to her, that she hadn't been living with her friend Ricki while she was in Rome. The outcome was Kate was told that she would never work for Miss Bluebell again. I saw a bit of a quandary here. Everyone knew that Vera and Giorgio, the set designer, had had a relationship. Did that mean that Vera wouldn't work for Miss Bluebell again, either?

That same day I went to the hairdressers. Although my trips to the hairdressers were simply to get my dark roots bleached, my hair always had to have a blueish rinse, to make sure it didn't come out yellow, a constant problem with bleached hair. This rinse tended to be a little different every time, so I always left the hairdresser with a different colored head of hair. As I so rarely went to the same hairdresser twice, there was no continuity and, as my language skills were truly basic, there was no hope of my communicating the subtleties of hair color, it was always a toss of the coin what shade of blonde I came out. That day, I left the hairdressers with a dark shade of mouse, plus the hairdresser had done terrible things to the texture of my hair: it frizzed like it had never frizzed before. I quickly returned to the hotel intent upon tidying it up by flattening it and pinning it into a French pleat and then coating it with lots of hair spray. First, I combed it outwards, in all directions, including over my eyes and nose. That was when I discovered I'd left my hairpins at the theater, so I sat down and wrote letters, waiting for Annie to return to the hotel, as I was certain she must have some. Eventually the girls returned, shrieking when they saw me. Vera followed them in to find out the cause of the uproar. (She was always trying to avert the inevitable complaints from the hotel that resulted from the noise we generated). She took one look at me, stalked out of the room and yelled back that she'd "finished with the whole bloody lot of us."

At this point in the contract, with physically tiring one-night stands ahead of us, ill health became an issue, and at times in Florence there were quite a few dancers off stage. This was not good for the quality of the show, but, of course, it was a diversion that tended to liven up an otherwise boring performance. Gabriele had injured his leg, and Luciano came down with the flu. Sylvia was off because she had gastroenteritis, and Jenny fell down coming out of the hairdressers and pulled a ligament so could do very little dancing. The doctor told Jenny she needed complete rest. Vera gave her nominal sympathy, and before a very strenuous number would say, "I suppose you'd better not do this number." Regarding Sylvia, Vera told her that she was fetching the doctor who would give her an injection to make it possible for her to work. The doctor did indeed come, but, luckily for Sylvia, confirmed that it was impossible for her to work.

Vera was having a hard time because of all this. She was in tears in the dressing room, telling us that we didn't have the team spirit, and that we didn't know how lucky we were to be Bluebells, and that we thought we were on holiday and— the ultimate insult—that we didn't have "the feeling of show-business." Then she gave us the news that Luciano, freshly down with the flu, wouldn't be in the *Finalissimo*, and instead of giving us some pointers on how the number would be re-choreographed, told us to work out the necessary changes to the number by ourselves, because she wasn't going to!

Jenny's replacement Stella arrived: she came from Bude in Cornwall and was a new Bluebell. She was definitely smaller than Jenny, so the costumes would fit her better! Jenny had to teach her all the dances. They started work that day and Stella picked it up fast.

Now that we'd completed twenty one-night stands (since the beginning of the tour) we were informed we would receive additional pay for each one-night stand. A one-night stand would now be defined as one or two days in one location. This past week we'd earned £1,000 extra.

Guido, of the vocal quartet, was now regularly asking me out—he must've fallen out with Carol yet again. He gave me an ultimatum: I could go out with him, which meant sleeping with him most nights, or have him repeatedly asking, with the curious addition of growling noises, whenever I passed him, on or off stage. In the previous year's show, he had teamed up with a girl quite early in the contract. They had special looks they gave to each other during the show which signaled whether she would be going to his room that night. The relationship was reported to Miss Bluebell and the girl was fired.

That night he was back with Carol and the whole thing was a bit embarrassing for her as word had traveled that he wanted to be dating me. She didn't speak to me for a few days, but I spent one evening teasing her, insisting she talk, and she softened.

Guido was not my only complication. During the show one night, the girls told me they had seen Paulo, my admirer from San Remo, back at the hotel. I didn't believe them until I returned to the hotel, and there he was. He stayed for a couple of days, and together we saw some of the local sights. The day before he left, he gave me a heart-shaped gold charm to be added to my new charm bracelet, along with a marriage proposal. It seemed his goal was to become engaged to a Bluebell from the *Dapporto Spettacolo* each year! Worse, he seemed to think that living on a Texaco oil tanker would appeal to me and wanted me to join him on his ship. I turned him down, and at the time I thought how bizarre it was that he thought a life at sea with him would be a more attractive proposition than moving to Canada, which he'd always known was my plan. I thought, not for the first time, that Italian men saw no humiliation or embarrassment in being rejected. "Nothing ventured, nothing gained," appeared to be their motto.

Finally, the end of the tour was announced on the notice board: May 7th.

Much to our annoyance, we started having daily rehearsals again, as Stella needed to be brought into the show. The first number she learned was the Presentation, and that night she performed in the show. I'd been told that it was "bad theater" to watch an understudy when he or she plays a part for the first time. Not so in the *Dapporto Spettacolo*. Nearly all the cast came into the wings to watch. The poor girl must've been so nervous, but she did a good job. After the show I went to dinner with her. She'd only been with us a few days, but the other girls couldn't stand her. Jenny didn't like her; said she was whiney, and it seemed that the other girls had adopted Jenny's opinion. Because I'd hardly spoken to her, I'd held voicing, or even coming to, an opinion. Anyway, I felt sorry for her, suddenly pushed into a world like this, so different from anything she'd experienced before, and among twelve girls who already knew each other so well.

Stella knew all the numbers well enough after a week, so it was time for Jenny to leave. We would all be leaving Florence on the same day. Jenny was heading home to England to prepare for her wedding, first going to Torino to meet her future in-laws, while we were leaving Florence to set out on several weeks of one-night stands.

As the day got close, Sylvia, Kate, and I were saddened; we were going to miss Jenny, and it was around this time that we were all thinking we wanted to see England again. Alice was already describing how wonderful the White Cliffs were going to look from the ferry when we were headed home. I echoed the sentiment, although I had found that I didn't generally suffer from homesickness: there were always people around, we were always busy, and the constant traveling was distracting.

On the day we left Florence, Jenny's train left forty minutes before ours, so we went to see her off. Annie and I decided to take her some flowers. We were late arriving at the station, checked on the time with the flower seller, and found that the train should've already left, three minutes before. We rushed down the platform, pushed the flowers into Jenny's hands and said goodbye. The train pulled away, carrying away a tearful Jenny, with us waving like mad.

CHAPTER TWELVE

NAPOLI AND VENEZIA

During the next two and a half weeks we performed the show in fifteen towns, traveling coast to coast, first by train, but then, as the towns we appeared in became more inaccessible, by bus. The whole company was with us, including the performers, backstage workers, dressers, orchestra, and even the pets.

On occasion we'd sleep in one hotel over several nights, traveling by bus to a different town each day to perform the show. This was an effort. After long hours on the bus, we'd arrive in time to prepare for the performance, have a meal immediately afterward and in the early hours of the morning head back to our hotel, getting into bed around 6:30 a.m. But the audiences loved us.

It wasn't unusual for our daily quota of sleep to be split into two or three segments. We'd be up early for the train— usually the slow train; the express train, which left later in the day, was more expensive so we never took it—sleep on the train and catch a few hours in the hotel before the show. Then we'd grab a few more hours of sleep in the hotel after the show before we headed back out to the train station around 8 a.m.

When traveling by bus, we'd sleep on the way to the town where the theater was located, sleep on our way back to the town where our hotel was located, and then several hours at the hotel.

I became adept at sleeping soundly even when I wasn't in a bed. It was March, and trains and buses were rarely warm when we first climbed aboard them. First, I'd wrap a scarf around my head, making sure my head stayed snug. Then I looked after my feet. I had a large, brown leather bag, shaped like a horse-feed bag with a drawstring around the top, a gift from my mother. I'd take off my shoes, put on thick socks, put my feet in the bag, and pull the drawstring up around my ankles. My feet remained warm, and the moment I felt the motion of the bus or train, I was asleep.

Now that we were traveling once more, the inevitable occurred. Several girls developed gastroenteritis. It wasn't surprising considering the number of hotel rooms, shared bathrooms, dressing rooms, restaurants, trains, train stations, and buses we frequented.

Sylvia was ill and not going on stage for any of her numbers, which wasn't good for the show (and especially not good for me, as I had to cha-cha-cha/wiggle in my huge towel, solo, across the stage in the shower number.)

Then, that same week at the theater, Jessie, returning to the dressing room from the bathroom, looking ghastly, announced she'd vomited. Vera, instead of showing concern, said, "Good, now you'll feel better." To be fair, Vera must've been nervous that Jessie was also coming down with gastroenteritis, which might've resulted in two dancers off the stage.

Happily, Jessie quickly recovered. "It was the ice cream," or so she said.

After she missed the show for several days, Sylvia asked Vera if she could go ahead to Naples, where we'd be appearing for six days, and spend the intervening week recuperating rather than traveling with the show. A phone call was made to Paris, and Miss Bluebell gave the plan her blessing.

The night before Sylvia left for Naples (and we left for more one-night stands) Vera gave us a lecture, telling us we were now to sit with her and Deanna at mealtimes and not rush to a table by ourselves. She added that we must do as she says at the theater, and at all other times when we are a "troupe." And finally, she informed us that she had asked Miss Bluebell to completely break up our troupe after the tour; so, as far as "company" was concerned, we could now go out with whom we liked. (I doubted that that sentiment would last.)

The next morning Sylvia came with us to the station, and we said goodbye to her. She was on her way to Naples, while we caught the train for Riccioni, the next stop on the tour. After a few days Vera checked in with her at the *pensione* in Naples; she was improving, which brought about a sigh of relief all around. It meant she wouldn't be going home and we, therefore, wouldn't be needing yet another replacement.

One week later, the rest of us (all but Sylvia) were on our way to Naples, a twelve-hour journey across the country from our last stop in Ascoli Piceno. I'd been looking forward to Naples since my arrival in Italy. In my mind it epitomized Italy: the Mediterranean Sea, fishing boats in the harbor, Mount Vesuvius, Pompeii, the Isle of Capri and Sorrento. Rome may have had its seven hills and its antiquities, but Naples was the star. I was ready to be enthralled by everything I saw.

When, after a long day, we approached Naples, not one girl was disappointed as we all strained to get our first look out of the train window. What we saw was spectacular. It was late in the day, the sun was setting, and the sky was the brightest shade of crimson with streaks of gold. And against this backdrop, Mount Vesuvius was silhouetted, and the lights of the city lay below, shining like tiny stars.

We would be in Naples six days, and I was going to be very busy. I had my job, of course, but I also hoped to do some sightseeing plus I needed to complete a list of "must-dos." During the previous two weeks I'd had a couple of personal mishaps: I'd left my reading glasses on a train and, more significantly, a very large filling had fallen out of my right incisor, a tooth at the front of my mouth, leaving a gap that showed when I talked or smiled, so I needed both a dentist and an optician. Also, I wanted to find a Cunard office. This was the last major city we'd be visiting on the tour, the last one where I could expect to find a Cunard office, and I planned on paying the final portion of my boat ticket to Canada. I also had plans to visit with some family friends, Vivian and Ann Morgan, from Birmingham.

On Day One I set out to work on my to-do list. The owners of the *pensione* had given me recommendations for an optician and dentist, but first I visited the Cunard office and paid the final portion of my boat fare. I was really going to Canada; my future was set!

The visit to the optician was less successful. I needed an eye test and a lens prescription, but I couldn't get help with that. The language barrier was just too much. I understood I was not in the right kind of shop and I didn't get any assistance in locating anyone who could help me. Now that we were no longer doing one-night stands, my large suitcase was once more in my possession and I was able to retrieve my back-up glasses, which I'd had since I was about fourteen. They would do until I was back in England.

Next, the dentist; a would-be Romeo, who was mostly eager for my company, even if he had to fill my tooth to get it. At my first appointment, he looked in my mouth, where the work was obviously needed, made an appointment to see me the next day and asked if he could see me after the show that night. I assured him that I always went straight home after the show. (Why didn't I just say, "no"? Did I think it was my job to protect the Italian male's fragile self-esteem, or did I think he'd get angry? In any case, none of us ever did.)

The next day I returned for my second appointment. Despite being twenty minutes late I was met with smiles. He filled the tooth, and instead of telling me, "Don't bite on it for two hours," he asked me out for lunch. I told him I was seeing friends. On the following day I saw him for the final appointment. I asked him what I owed him, and he said he'd done the work "from the heart—for a *bella donna*." He then took my hand, kissed it several times, and implored me to let him take me for a meal should I return to Naples in the summer.

I saw my new English friends, Vivian and Ann, and their two young sons, several times during the week. (Through the years I'd met Vivian's mother several times at my grandmother's house, but I didn't know that she had a son who lived in Naples until my mother had written that he and his wife, probably eager see someone from home, would like to meet me.)

We would meet at one of their favorite restaurants, one in which they assured me they'd inspected the kitchens—which they told me was an important precursor to frequenting a Napolese eating establishment—and as the week progressed, they'd take me up to their apartment in the hills above Naples, from which there was a glorious view of the city and the bay and feed me English staples such as Marmite and boiled eggs. It struck me as unusual to find a young English family settled in Naples. Vivian told me that in World War II, when the British army, fighting its way up Italy, reached Naples, he'd spent his first night sleeping between two palm trees on the sea front, and as he lay there, had vowed that after the war he'd return there to live. It took him a good many years to do it, but two years prior, he and his family made the move.

My visits with them were visits to an isle of normalcy where people were awake when it was light and slept when it was dark. I listened to recordings of West End musicals, helped with the dishes, laughed about life in the Bluebells and reminisced about Northfield, where both Vivian and I had grown up. And just as I enjoyed visiting their world, they were curious to know more about mine. After I described the way we lived, with all the Bluebell rules that accompanied that life, Vivian enquired, "Do they leave your souls untouched?"

I also managed to fit in some sightseeing. Sylvia and I took a morning tour of Pompeii. This was early spring in the days before the cruise ships called in at Naples and we enjoyed a quiet, peaceful morning sauntering around the ancient town—an ideal way to enjoy it.

On another day, Carol, Stella, and I visited the Isle of Capri, calling in at Sorrento on the way and also visiting the Blue Grotto, the color of the water reminding me of copper sulphate crystals from high school chemistry class. A magical and unique experience.

That night, when we walked into the theater, we learned some shocking news: Mr. Libo had been killed in a car accident in southern France. We'd seen him only three weeks earlier, in La Spezia, where he'd lectured us on the sins of making excessive noise in hotels; he'd been receiving complaints. Now there would be no more lectures and no more watching out for his bald head in the audience. We girls kept our thoughts to ourselves and there was very little discussion. Without a doubt I was shocked, but I felt no sorrow; the fact that he was gone from our lives seemed a positive; he was not a person that I'd miss. Nevertheless, I was definitely concerned for Miss Bluebell because she had lost her business manager and it was my understanding that it had been Mr. Libo's responsibility to negotiate the contracts for the organization. I wondered how she was going to manage without him. The organization appeared to me to be small because both Miss Bluebell and Mr. Libo appeared to be personally available to each of the dancers. In answer to my enquiries, I was told that Patrick, their son (who'd also been in the accident but was expected to fully recover) had been helping out over the last few years so I was hopeful he had sufficient knowledge to help her keep things going.

The ensuing years have proven that Miss Bluebell coped well and carried on just fine; she obviously had not been dependent on her husband, and to the Bluebell Girl of today, Mr. Libo is merely a note in history.

When Mr. Libo visited last, he and Vera had talked privately about Kate and Deanna. Both were having relationships with members of the company, so neither would work for the Bluebell organization again. It was final.

The upshot of this was that it was now more difficult for Vera to control the rest of us, particularly because the whole company was now traveling together all the time. When she insisted that we sit four to a compartment in the train, we bristled: we liked sitting with our friends. When she insisted that we sit at her table in the restaurants, we headed in another direction, again with our friends. Only the very youngest, and those girls with the least seniority, and hence the least job security, did as she bid. This meant that only Jessie, Stella, and sometimes Annie and Alice, obeyed her when her directions seemed unreasonable. Kate and Deanna went their own way with their boyfriends, leaving five of us with relative independence. Vera was unhappy, and at one point declared, as she had twice before on the tour, that she was "washing her hands of us," a declaration that was met with glee.

Another interesting development: imagine our surprise when we arrived in Naples and found that Vera and Deanna were not staying in our *pensione*; they'd been booked elsewhere. This had never occurred before. True, our *pensione* appeared to be full (I was sharing a room with Carol and Stella), but even so, it was odd. Why weren't two of the older girls in the other *pensione* and Vera with us, keeping tabs on Jessie, who was "under license"?

I suspected the simplest of reasons: Giorgio, her scenic designer boyfriend was visiting from Rome, and Vera needed more freedom and privacy. Or maybe she thought it would be good for us to see what life was like without a Captain.

As the week passed the girls freely socialized with the men in the company and, at all hours of the night, cars would be driven past the *pensione,* a horn would honk, and girls would leave the *pensione* to join their dates. On at least one occasion, the men came into the *pensione* in the middle of the night unannounced and uninvited. Anselmo, of the vocal quartet, with Guido in tow for moral support, arrived in our room at 4 a.m. Anselmo wanted Stella to go with him to his hotel. She was tired. She'd already turned him down when he'd asked her during dinner, and here he was trying again. We sent them packing.

Jessie, who was only seventeen, was soon dating Enzo, who was approaching middle age; Stella, who had just had her eighteenth birthday, and had been a Bluebell for all of four weeks, was infatuated with Anselmo. A very poor choice in my eyes, as he was not only sleeping regularly with her, but also once a week with Monica and, so I was told, engaged to a Bluebell from the previous year's Dapporto tour.

After our week in Naples, our next stop would be Venice and after that, Salerno. A quick look at a map of Italy confirms that that wasn't very efficient. Venice was a day's train ride north of Naples and Salerno less than thirty miles south of Naples, but I knew by now that we weren't following the "efficiency model," but rather one of the "available theater."

As usual, the train left very early, so we traveled on almost no sleep, and for the first time and not the last, I slept up high over the seats, in the luggage rack. I wanted to stretch out my body, and as long as the metal bar in the center of the rack didn't come in contact with my hip, I was reasonably comfortable.

We would be appearing in the Casino on the Venice Lido, rather than in the City of Venice—so, not the picture-book Venice—but I was still thrilled to be heading there. We took the water bus from the Venice railway station, down the Grand Canal past St. Mark's and the Doge's Palace, and across a wide expanse of water to the Lido. There we caught regular taxis and it seemed to me that we'd landed in a place similar to a wealthy suburb of Birmingham, with many dignified, early twentieth-century villas. What was different was that there were fenced off private beaches at the end of the roads. The place had a deserted appearance; the Lido was a summer resort, and this wasn't summer.

We'd been booked into an inexpensive *pensione*, and soon discovered why the cost was low. It was March, and this was northern Italy—Venice was cold, and our rooms had neither heat nor hot running water. The next afternoon we went to the theater for a rehearsal, but the stage wasn't ready, and instead we were sent, via taxi, back to the old *pensione* to hurriedly (very hurriedly, while the taxis waited outside) pack our bags as we were moving to a *pensione* closer to the Casino, and hopefully, warmer. Vera was again housed elsewhere, but the boys, surprisingly, were housed with us.

After the show on opening night, there was a social event at the Casino which the whole company was required to attend. There was a band playing and drinks were served, and it was dull. I assume it was a promotional "do," or a thank-you to us for making the effort to come to this odd little corner of the world in the off-season. Either way, it wasn't explained to us, and I saw it as just a lot of unnecessary dressing up. In order to appear at such after-show events, we dancers had to remove our stage make-up and the general grime of performing in less-than-clean costumes, and then immediately apply day makeup, smart hairdos and good-looking clothes—a lot of effort for a drink and music at two o'clock in the morning!

Some of the dressing rooms at the Casino had no heat, so the actors, members of the vocal quartet and male dancers signed a petition: "No heat—No work." The show always began with the Overture, followed immediately by a number featuring the quartet and the boys. Each night, while the Overture was playing, the boys and quartet would stand behind the curtain ready to start their number. That night, because the boys and quartet were honoring the petition, they didn't go on stage for that first number. Augusto, the electrician, whose responsibility it was to tell the Orchestra Director that "backstage" was ready for the show to begin, assumed that the quartet and boys were on stage (they'd been there every other night since Milan) and signaled to the Orchestra Director to begin the Overture. While the Overture was in progress, Augusto realized his mistake, and went through the curtains, leaned over into the orchestra pit, and told the Orchestra Director to stop playing. The orchestra completed the Overture, and then there was ten minutes of silence. (We were aware of the silence, as we heard it over the loudspeaker in our dressing room but had no idea what it was all about.) In the meantime, the quartet and boys learned that the actors were going to renege on the petition so, begrudgingly, they moved to the stage to perform their first number. So, the petition had failed, the Overture was repeated, and the show went on, with no heat.

That wasn't the end: between the two shows we heard a loud noise outside our dressing room, and when we went out to investigate, we found Anselmo fighting with Augusto, the electrician, with Bruno, the carpenter, and Enzo, the actor, trying to separate them. We never understood the details behind this altercation, but it certainly livened up our evening. It was getting late in the tour and it seemed tempers were fraying.

That same evening, we had our own drama. Nearing the end of an argument, to make a special point, Vera grabbed Sophie by the arm, and shouted, "You're a bitch and look like a prostitute on stage."

"Do you know what *you* look like on stage?" Sophie responded.

"Yes, I do know. Twice my age!"

The argument ended in a draw, with both combatants vowing, "I'm writing to Miss Bluebell," and so, once more, all was quiet in the dressing room. But the next night Sophie had developed a bruise on her arm from where Vera had grabbed her. In a previous tour, Vera had got into trouble for hitting a girl, so I supposed we should feel lucky that a bruise is all the damage she'd caused so far.

It was Easter Week. It started well, with chocolate Easter eggs from Vera and only one show on Easter Day, but our joy was premature; we had two shows on Monday. Things bucked up on Tuesday; there was only one show, the sun was shining, and it was a beautiful day so Sylvia, Sophie, and I went across the lagoon into Venice. It was wonderful being away from the dreary Lido. We had lunch and went to the movies, but first we sat over coffee in St. Mark's Square where we were filmed for *Pathé News*. We loved being filmed, and yes, it only ever happened to me when I was with Sophie.

Later in the week the weather was still good so Sophie, Alice, Annie, Gabriele, and I went sunbathing on the beach of the deserted Hotel Excelsior, the five-star hotel on the Lido. The private beach was closed off to the public but the workmen, who were cleaning the bathing huts for the summer season, let us in. I didn't own a bikini so I borrowed one of Sophie's for the afternoon: my first public appearance in a bikini. This was the day we embarked on our plan to return to England with suntans. Within a few weeks we'd be back in our home communities, and in that setting we were celebrities so, of course, wanted to look our best. In England there was a certain prestige to having a tan, especially when it wasn't the height of summer, as it meant that you had both sufficient clout in your place of employment to take a vacation during the winter months, and the means to travel abroad. Hence the importance to us that we get off that train at Victoria Station with a tan! Fortunately, the remainder of the tour was going to be in southern Italy and Sicily, and often near the beach, so we knew there'd be opportunity for sunbathing.

Sunday was the end of the Venice run and we performed two shows. After the second show, we ate dinner at the Casino, and took a water taxi from the Casino in the middle of the night, over to the Venice Railway Station to catch a 6:15 a.m. train for Salerno. The previous day we'd packed our large suitcases; we wouldn't be seeing them again until we were in Paris—in four weeks' time. The good news was that we were told to send our rehearsal kits, which meant no more full rehearsals.

In the water taxi, most of us sat outside so we could get our last view of St. Mark's. We didn't ever expect to see it again. Headscarves and slacks were the outfit of the day; for such a long trip we had special dispensation. We still wore make-up, of course, and were still very tall so we were still recognizable as Bluebells. We had two hours at the station before the train was to leave. The majority of the girls made themselves comfortable in the darkened compartments, readying themselves for the fifteen-hour journey. Sylvia and I, knowing we wouldn't sleep until the train was in motion, sat and chatted in the station cafe watching the early morning activity on the Grand Canal. I was still thrilled to be in Venice.

CHAPTER THIRTEEN

HEADING SOUTH

Over the course of the tour, we performed in fifty-two towns, and we visited thirty percent of those towns in the final month—a month of almost continuous one-night stands. We now routinely performed a show, had a meal, slept a few hours in a hotel, and moved on, arriving in a new town the following day in time to perform the show. Now the backstage workers had a twenty-four hour schedule. When we were sleeping, they were driving to the next town, where we'd find them napping backstage. There was a scene in the show that took place in a Salvation Army Hostel. The props included bunkbeds, so when the men weren't working and the bunkbeds weren't needed on stage, we'd find the men fast asleep on them.

But first we had to get from Venice to Salerno. It was the most miserable train journey I'd ever taken. I was up in the luggage rack but couldn't get comfortable so got little sleep and was very happy when we arrived in Salerno at last. The good news was that, as we'd been traveling south all day, the climate was completely different from that of Venice; it was warm, and that night we lay in our beds with French windows open wide, listening to the crickets.

Before we settled down to sleep, while we were still chatting with friends, Vera visited our room. We'd be in Salerno for two days; the first would be a rest day (for which Vera had plans), and there'd be a show on the following day. On our rest day, she wanted the four of us in the room to go with her to Positano, a coastal town forty miles north of Salerno. An old boyfriend, Ruggero, had invited her to his villa and asked her to bring four girls along. She asked me, Alice, and Annie (I don't recall who the fourth was). I was enthusiastic about being included, but Alice and Annie were not. They wanted to stay in Salerno with their boyfriends, members of the company. I was in money-saving mode: a rest day meant a £2,000 reduction in salary, so a trip to a beautiful town, plus meals thrown in, sounded very agreeable.

The next day, three of us plus Vera (Alice had outwitted Vera and remained in Salerno) were picked up and driven to Positano. It turned out to be an unforgettable day. Positano has to be up there amongst the most glorious spots on earth. The coastal road that led there was incredibly winding, but the reward was the views of the Mediterranean, which were breathtaking. As soon as we arrived, we were taken for a meal at a restaurant where we sat out on a large terrace, overlooking the sea. There was a lattice roof over the terrace from which wisteria blooms hung, and petals dropped in both our food and wine throughout the meal. It was magical! I thought I was in heaven.

After lunch we climbed lots of stone steps (2,134 to be exact) up to Ruggero's cliffside villa. We entered through a doorway in a whitewashed wall and found ourselves in a small courtyard. Off the courtyard to the right was a door to the upper rooms of the house; a bathroom and, I assumed, one or more bedrooms. To the left of the courtyard was an archway facing the sea, leading to a flight of stone steps which led to the lower level of the house: a living-room and a kitchen, which is where we were headed. Each of these rooms had an open fireplace, and the living room had a balcony overlooking the sea. The villa was built on a ledge cut into a steep cliff-face and it appeared to be built of the same rock as the cliff. As I looked out over the balcony, I could see the roofs of other villas which were tucked in on other ledges across the cliff-face. Looking down, the sea seemed quite close, but that was an illusion because, when fishing boats came into view, they were mere specks of light a long, long way below.

We sat around with drinks, and once the town's long lunch hour had ended and the shops were open, we walked down the many steps and did some shopping. I was very keen on buying a bikini, and because not every town had bikinis for sale in 1961, this beach resort was my opportunity. The one I chose didn't quite fit me and needed to be altered. The shop owner took me into the back of the shop to her sewing area and, to my surprise I found myself in a cave, with roughhewn rock walls! There, I tried on the swimsuit and she determined how much to take in. She sat down at her sewing machine, and made the alteration. Then, with our shopping completed the four of us headed back up to Ruggero's villa and all those 2,134 steps.

During the evening, additional men arrived, friends of Ruggero. They were all showing off for each other and took little notice of us, and from their behavior and conversation we concluded that their *raison d'être* was to sponge off Ruggero.

We understood that all the men were "in spaghetti," and Ruggero was the managing director of a pasta factory. Their showing off got completely out of hand, and at one point they were throwing a full bottle of cognac to each other round the room, which, not surprisingly, eventually broke. I looked absolutely aghast, to which Ruggero responded, "It's OK—we'll open another one."

The men left it until late to think about dinner, and the shops were already shut. That was no problem. They simply got a shop owner out of bed and obtained the necessary food, which somehow found its way up to the villa. In time, the men cooked a meal. It was served, enjoyed, and we spent the rest of the evening sitting around the open fire listening to records, ending it all with the drive back to Salerno, and bed at 3 a.m.

Two days later we took the train to Cosenza, a town surrounded by mountains. Stepping out onto the platform I noticed a woman of indeterminate age, with a very weathered face, a shawl around her shoulders, balancing a basket on her head, and inside the basket lay a shopping bag and an umbrella. This was my first glimpse of a peasant, the people who lived in the hillvillages of southern Italy. Seeing her gave me a jolt; I'd touched down in a different country, in a different era.

The next day, on our way to Catanzaro, our bus had mechanical problems. When we realized that the driver was attempting to make a 180-degree turn on the mountain road, a road with a sharp drop off, we all objected, very loudly. The driver, wisely, changed his plans, and drove the crippled bus on to the next village where we waited for a replacement. Sitting in the bus, we were the subject of great curiosity by the local population. First the children came out to stare, dozens of them, and soon the women followed—but there were never any signs of working age men. (I have since read that they were away working the land.)

During our travels around the south over the next few weeks, this was repeated at every stop we made. It's possible the villagers knew who we were, because we'd see posters from the show glued on walls in tiny communities many miles from where we were to perform, but it was just as likely that we were a curiosity because we were outsiders, just as they were a curiosity to us.

That evening, following the *Finalissimo*, when we danced around the *passerella* enjoying our final round of applause from the audience, I was halfway round when the line of girls ahead of me came to a sudden halt and the music trailed away, sort of muffled. Monica had fallen into the orchestra pit and landed on the first trumpeter! It was quite a drop but luckily her costume had lots of underskirts, and she landed softly. The audience stood up, everyone on stage surged forward, and cameras flashed. When we went round on the next *passerella* (minus Monica and Vera, who'd gone to see how Monica was faring) we received a greater applause than even Dapporto (who, let's face it, was supposed to be the star of the show)—all at Monica's expense. There was no word on the trumpeter.

As we moved further south, we became more and more aware of the differences between the south and the rest of Italy. For example, we couldn't understand what people said and they couldn't understand us. We learned that many of the locals were speaking a different language from the one that we'd learned: probably Neapolitan or Sicilian, and both languages came with several dialects. And it didn't help that we not only spoke a different language from the locals, but we had also learned Italian with a Milanese accent.

We now frequently saw peasants, any time we passed through rural communities. In the late afternoon it was common to see a man leading a donkey, packed with dried tree branches, with a goat on a rope trailing behind. He would have taken the donkey out for the day to carry home the brush he'd collected, fuel for heating and cooking, taking the goat along to graze. Another common sight was women collecting water at the village faucet, then walking home with pitchers balanced on their heads. And a scene I saw only once but is embedded in my memory: a peasant woman sitting in the doorway of her meager cottage, working on embroidery.

Many of the men in Italy who crossed our paths, men we didn't know personally, treated us in ways we found extremely offensive. Their behavior ranged from honking car horns as we walked down the street or surrounding us as we walked anywhere. Some would put their eye to the keyhole when we were in the "loo" at the theaters or in our bedrooms at the *pensiones*. The men in the south of the country differed from the men in the north in that, in the north, when a culprit was caught in the act, he was shamefaced, whereas in the south he merely tittered.

Another aggravation was that on Sundays, when there were two shows, waiters would bring us food from neighborhood restaurants. The rule was that they should never come into our dressing room unannounced, but it was not uncommon for these waiters to barge in unannounced, hoping to glimpse a bra or a fishnetted thigh, even though it meant they would be screamed at. Apparently, it was worthwhile to suffer the indignity of twelve women screaming at you in order to have a glimpse of female skin.

The last town where we played before heading for Sicily was Vibo Valentia. There was no *passerella* at the theater, so Vera insisted that we have a rehearsal before the show. This was unusual, but prudent. She'd discontinued holding "position" rehearsals on one-night stands, and we would routinely just go on stage for each number and hope for the best. By this late date on the tour, the dancers on the front row had a lot of experience at spacing themselves on odd-shaped stages, and we dancers in the back row were adept at positioning ourselves in the spaces behind. But a theater with no *passerella* raised new issues, so Vera had to re-work some of the choreography.

A few nights earlier, in Reggio Calabria, we'd met a group of young men who were actually well-behaved: friends of the son of the theater director. On our last night on the mainland, they turned up and took us to dinner once more. After the meal, we said thank you and goodbye, boarded a bus waiting for us at the theater, and were taken to a train station. There, the whole company, front and backstage, waited for many hours for the train that would ferry us to Sicily, the men, as usual, playing cards. Whenever I dropped off to sleep, I'd be awakened by a *mechanisti* who had won some money thumping his fist on a nearby table.

As I sat there, for those many hours, I thought to myself that this was exactly what I had always envisioned a theatrical life to be: being part of a close community, with few complaints about the discomfort, certain that we were the chosen few—after all, wasn't there stiff competition for each of our jobs?—and with the knowledge that none of us wanted to be anywhere else.

The train crossed over to Sicily on a rail barge, and after much *shunting* and *clanging*, we found ourselves on the regular train line heading east to Catania, arriving there at 12:30 p.m. that same day. I had slept the whole journey and that evening we performed our first show in Sicily.

Before the show, instead of taking my usual nap at the hotel, I joined Annie, Carol, Guido, Alice, and Gabriele on the beach, where we bravely faced a brisk wind to work on our tans. It was cold. The sun was shining, but cold is cold, so we soon called it quits, put on our street clothes and moved into a bar for hot drinks. The girls were now openly socializing with members of the company. Vera was still doing her best to keep us apart, with little success. Earlier that day, when we'd been on the ferry, poor Vera had been beside herself when she'd checked into our compartment and found Guido nuzzling up to Carol, both fast asleep.

The show that night was uneventful, but not everyone was in a good mood. The *mechanistas* had made the ferry crossing with up to nine in a compartment and, upon arrival in Catania, had to work immediately, to get the stage ready for the show. They were dead tired, so we stayed away from them. However, we felt differently about Dapporto, when, during the evening, he chastised Alice telling her to "put some spirit" into her dancing. What nerve, after us not having seen a bed for nearly forty-eight hours!

The next afternoon, around eight of us, members of the company and dancers, celebrated Annie's birthday with a beach party at a local restaurant. The weather was much warmer than the previous day, so, ignoring the fact that bikinis were illegal in Sicily, we sunbathed for several hours, after which we had a meal and listened to music from a jukebox until around 5 p.m.

After returning to the *pensione* I bumped into Stella who'd not been at the party. Together we wandered around the shops and I purchased more clothing: an off-white pleated skirt and an off-white handbag. I was starting to put together my summer wardrobe, intending to arrive in Kingston (the college town in Canada where I was headed) as the best-dressed ex-dancer they'd ever met. That afternoon I'd spent £10,000, but I considered it money well spent. I loved looking good, and I could afford the extravagance, as I'd done a good job of saving during the tour.

There had been a downside to the strict budget I'd set myself, which had cut into my social life. I'd often eaten alone in a less expensive restaurant than the others, and on many occasions, I'd not joined them for a meal after the show. It had definitely set me apart, and I'd also lost some weight I didn't need to lose. Be that as it may, I was of the opinion that I'd found it relatively easy to save because I was one of the few Bluebells who'd lived independently prior to working for Miss Bluebell. For many of the girls, this was the first job they'd had after leaving school. I also had an exciting near-term goal: my new life in Canada.

To be clear, we were not encouraged to save money. We were encouraged to spend it on being well-dressed, well turned out, and being seen in the best places. However, as we came to the end of the tour, there was a common realization that the time had arrived for everyone to save, as all the girls would need money when they arrived home. If they were expecting to work for Miss Bluebell again it might be several months before they received the call that they were needed for another tour, or as a replacement dancer at the Lido or Stardust. Their predicament was similar if they were leaving the Bluebell fold and hoping to work for another employer. Even though a dancer with "Bluebell" on her resume would have no problem getting another job dancing, there would always be a gap between contracts.

I gathered that most of the girls would spend the period between contracts back in their parents' home. Alice and I were the only dancers who had another salable skill. We were both shorthand typists, and in 1961, in both London, where Alice was from, and Birmingham, you could be employed as a temp on the day after you applied to an agency.

From our limited perspective, we all liked Catania, a thriving city which reminded us of northern Italy. It was so different from the rest of the south. We saw shops with names that were familiar to us. We saw many Americans who were employed at the nearby oil refineries, presumably with high paying jobs. And the theater in which we were appearing was one of the most modern in Europe, built in 1954. The auditorium was huge, and each night we had full houses "plus standing." Closer to our hearts, our dressing room was luxurious: at one end it had a warm-up space, with a piano and practice barre, and leading off the dressing room was a bathroom with wash basins, toilets, and showers.

Unbelievable! Another thing we liked about Catania was that the men on the streets acted more respectfully towards us.

On our second day in Catania, Vera bumped into me in the hotel and asked if I had a few hours to spare the following day. Dapporto, Marisa, and the quartet were making a "demo" recording and wanted Vera and me to sing some "ooohs" in the background. (Vera and I were the unofficial "Bluebell singers." Vera had a two-note solo at the end of Marisa's song in the *Orientale*, and I was her understudy.) I said "yes" immediately. We had a short rehearsal in Sandro's (of the quartet) dressing room that evening, and the next day we met at the theater to make the recording. The orchestra was there, with Guido conducting. We stood at microphones in the auditorium near the orchestra pit and made quite a few recordings, and after each one all the singers walked half-way up the center-aisle to hear it replayed. I think it all went well and I loved the whole experience.

I knew that this was an experience to treasure, but it's only now that I realize what exceptional musical company I was keeping that day. In the ensuing years Sandro (Allesandro Allesandroni) wrote over forty movie scores, collaborating with Ennio Morricone and also working with Director Sergio Leone on spaghetti westerns. When you watch Clint Eastwood in those movies, it's Sandro you're hearing when you listen to the twangy guitar and the lone whistler. And the vocal group heard in the orchestrations is *I Cantori Moderni di Allesandroni*, Sandro's group that was an expansion of our vocal quartet.

Giulia, who I haven't mentioned, was the fourth member of the quartet, and the wife of Sandro. Giulia was pregnant—

very pregnant—a pregnancy which must've begun way back during rehearsals. She was getting more rotund by the day. The baby was due at the end of May and we'd been told that she'd leave the show after we left Venice. However, she was still with us and we now heard that she'd work until the end of the tour. Through the months, as her body had expanded, the dressers let out and redesigned her costumes as needed, but now she routinely wore a short cloak, always color coordinated with the three men's costumes. Giulia only came on stage for the quartet's vocal numbers and never at the end of either Act I or II, when she'd have to walk around the always somewhat precarious *passerella*. One wonders how she'd been existing on our schedule. Admittedly, she probably wasn't spending her afternoons sunbathing like us, but even so, she couldn't have been getting much sleep!

We next moved on to Palermo where we'd be staying for three days. That night at the theater I was told by various girls that they'd seen Paulo, my beau from San Remo, that evening. I was sure they were joking, but as the evening wore on, I unhappily realized that they weren't. I didn't particularly like being followed around Italy, and I felt sure his enthusiasm was based solely on the fact that I was a Bluebell—and what's more, I suspected that as far as Paulo was concerned, any one of us would have done just as nicely! Paulo told me his ship, the *Texaco Iowa*, was docked in Palermo. I assumed he was telling the truth. So, for my time in Palermo I had an escort, and I visited a handful of small neighboring resorts and enjoyed meals until the early hours of the morning in lovely outdoor restaurants, which, for a girl raised in the English climate, were a great novelty. Ignoring my original annoyance at Paulo's persistence, I thoroughly enjoyed the special treatment.

There was a downside, of course. Being fêted by Paulo meant that I lost sleep, and I was already sleep deprived. It was very nice to be taken out to lovely restaurants before and after the show, but I needed sleep more than I needed fine dining. Also, spending much of my time with a man who wasn't connected to the show resulted in my being less focused on my job. On our last day in Palermo, I had been taken to a restaurant way across town before the show. I was in the middle of a discussion comparing the English, American, and Italian education systems when I realized that it was 8:15 p.m. and I had to be in the theater at 8:30 p.m. I jumped into a taxi, first heading to the hotel to collect my things, then to the theater, where I arrived about ten, quite unforgivable, or so we were always told, minutes late. At 9:05 p.m. I suddenly realized I'd left my tights in my bedroom. Back to the hotel, back to the theater and, thank heavens, I still made the show on time. When we left Palermo, I was relieved to leave Paulo and the *Texaco Iowa* behind.

Maybe to maintain freshness, and "keep us on our toes," Vera was now regularly holding short rehearsals. The show started around 9:15 p.m. and we had our rehearsals at around 5 p.m., to give us time for a meal before the show. When we arrived at the theater for the rehearsal, we would often find there was a movie showing in the theater, so we'd tip toe and talk in whispers as we walked across the stage behind the movie screen, locating our dressing rooms and becoming familiar with the layout of the backstage area. My guess is that the movie audience was none the wiser as the soundtrack was loud, and presumably covered up all the odd sounds that disseminated from the Bluebell activity.

With the tour so near the end you would think that there would be no more gossip, and no more occasions for Vera to get upset, but there was still lots going on. Relationships between the girls and members of the company were now increasingly out in the open, with Vera still relentless in her quest to contain the bad behavior.

By that time, Anselmo had switched to seeing Monica for a few days, only to quickly return his attentions to Stella after he'd found out that Monica was mostly interested in sleep.

The morning we left Caltanizetta for Syracuse we had a very early start, and it happened that Vera was up long before any of us. For some reason she went into Carol and Stella's room and found Stella sitting on the bed, nude, with Anselmo behind the door, almost nude. Vera withdrew, speechless, but then fumed all day. In the evening, when we were in the dressing room, she asked Stella, "What was Anselmo doing in your room this morning? I'm no fool you know."

"Oh, well you know, then!" Stella replied.

The rest of us girls overheard this conversation and, of course, found it funny. We could imagine the look of disbelief and/or disgust on Vera's face when she'd come upon Anselmo and Stella that morning, and our spirits were lifted for the whole evening. We weren't the kindest group of girls and there's no doubt we liked bad things to happen to Vera.

Not surprisingly, that evening there were some new edicts. Vera told Carol to stop sleeping with Guido, and in the future Stella and Carol were always to eat with her. In addition, Jessie was told to have nothing to do with Stella, because she was a bad influence. *Seems a little late for that*, I thought to myself.

I was still looking for ways to make my evenings more interesting, anything to alleviate the boredom caused by the repetitiveness of the show. Near the end of the tour, I invented a new distraction, one that kept me occupied for quite a few performances. In the *Orientale*, following our energetic pirouettes, we sat on the stage in a semi-circle around Marisa del Frate while she sang a solo. While she sang, we looked at her or into the audience, while maintaining our Mona Lisa smiles. What better conditions under which to attempt a mathematical calculation! I would, repeatedly, attempt to figure out how many performances we'd given throughout the tour. It was a complicated calculation, what with rest days, two shows every Sunday, and occasional travel days. I would picture the columns of numbers in my head and the "carries," and memorize the anomalies. On some days I'd almost get to the end of the calculation, then I'd have to start dancing, and all my work would be for naught. (Though I've still never completed the calculation, it must be around 260.)

The next day there was a day of *divertimento* for the Bluebell Girls, and Annie and I were the cause. The company was on its way to Messina, but Annie and I weren't! At the moment the train left at 12:10 p.m. Annie and I were sleeping peacefully. I awoke at 12:30 p.m. and quickly woke Annie and broke the dreadful news to her. We were horrified. No Bluebell *ever* missed the train! We fully expected Vera to arrive back from the station, looking for us, and prepared ourselves to face the full force of her wrath. But apparently, we hadn't been missed.

Once we got used to the idea that the train had left and everyone, except us, was on it, we began to see the whole disaster as funny. When *would* they miss us? On the steps in the Presentation? I'd had a good eight hours' sleep and felt better for it and was up to handling anything. So we made our way to the station and took the next train to Messina. Luckily it was a direct train, because I'm not sure we could have handled a transfer with our limited Italian vocabulary[2], and in any case, everyone spoke with a Sicilian dialect.

We had a meal at the station and before getting on the train, attempted to phone our hotel in Messina to leave a message for Vera, to let her know that we'd be on the next train. However, we gave up on this when we found that it took three-and-a-half hours for a call to be connected through to Messina—where was it going, via London and Paris?—while the train journey would only take three hours.

Usually we sat in reserved compartments, but as we weren't with the company, we had to share our compartment with the local citizenry. There we sat, two blonde young women, surrounded by Sicilian men who were unknown quantities. Thankfully, no one bothered us, and, in fact, the men all appeared completely disinterested. Even so, we were watching them, and there was a silent gasp from each of us when Annie elbowed me to draw my attention to the businessman sitting opposite. He was wearing a gun under his jacket. Our eyes

---

[2] Limited to all parts of theater costumes and street clothes and any and all catastrophes associated with clothing, such as, ripped, lost, broken-zip etc; food and how it should be cooked; ordering services from hotel personnel; communicating with backstage workers as necessary; and a working knowledge of insults to shout at men who attempted to touch us.

nearly popped out of our heads. We were two English girls and neither of us had ever seen a handgun before. We didn't need convincing; it was obvious we were sharing a compartment with at least one member of the Mafia.

The train drew into the Messina station and Vera was waiting for us on the platform. We were apprehensive regarding our welcome, but we needn't have worried. She wasn't particularly annoyed; probably just relieved. Later, we heard from the other girls how the morning had gone. All the girls had been pretty late for the train and it wasn't until the train had left the station that anyone realized we were missing. Vera was very upset at this discovery, with much screaming and tears coming from her compartment. In fact, it had been so raucous that the rest of the company had hung out of their compartments into the corridor to listen to her.

Thanks to Annie and me, Vera's day had not started well, and it didn't improve. Later, as we were gathering on stage for the afternoon's rehearsal, she asked Stella where she'd eaten.

"At a small restaurant," Stella responded.

"With whom?"

"Alone."

"I don't believe you," Vera said, and Stella quickly admitted that she'd been with Anselmo. To no one's surprise, Vera let fly.

I'd been delayed in the dressing room, doctoring a problem-pimple on Jessie's back, but heard it all. Vera called Stella "a little bitch," and Anselmo, who'd been playing the piano in the orchestra pit and listening to the conversation, decided to put in his two cents, telling Vera, "You're a lonely woman."

Vera responded, "Yes?"

"And inside, you're old," Anselmo said.

This, of course, was the ultimate insult to a woman whose livelihood depended on maintaining relative youth. It was also mean! Vera burst into a flood of tears, noisy tears, which we could hear up in the dressing room.

The upshot of the episode was that we didn't have a rehearsal, and I, having a generous heart, swapped my place in the dressing room with Stella, who normally sat next to Vera. Vera didn't dance much of the show that night, with no reason given.

The next night I shared a room with Sylvia. We slept until 2 p.m. The train left at 7 p.m. and we were on the train for the next thirteen hours, traveling back to the mainland, to Bari on the east coast.

CHAPTER FOURTEEN

HOMEWARD BOUND

hen we gathered at Messina railway station for our return to the mainland there were ten days of the tour remaining. We all had home on our minds, and it was the most frequent topic of conversation. That evening, however, the only topic of conversation was Monica's new German Shepherd puppy, which she wanted to take with her on the train. She'd been given it the previous day by a man she'd first met in Catania and who'd followed her to Messina.

Vera saw the puppy and, not surprisingly, threw a fit and told Monica that the puppy couldn't travel with her. Luciano stepped forward and offered to say the puppy was his, and would, therefore, be traveling with him. Vera had no authority over Luciano, so the puppy was allowed on the train. However, a problem soon arose, because Luciano became attached to the puppy and wanted to keep it. Monica was absolutely not going to stand for that, and with tears flowing, refused to part with it.

The next puppy problem arose eleven hours into our thirteen-hour journey, at 6 a.m. the following morning. The ticket inspector came around and demanded £4,400 for a ticket for the pup. Monica had no money, but still wouldn't give the dog to Luciano. She rationalized that she'd borrow money for train tickets and dog food and, when she arrived home in Brussels, she'd sell the puppy to pay off the debt. Though it made no sense, this was her plan, and she stuck with it. The puppy remained with us for the final few days of the tour.

We'd be appearing in three more towns—Brindisi, Foggia, and Pescara—and had been told that Miss Bluebell would visit us in Foggia. It seemed that it was her practice to have contact with the girls at the beginning and the end of a contract. She'd seen us on the day we arrived in Milan, and now would be seeing us in Foggia.

It didn't happen that way; instead, Miss Bluebell's son Patrick appeared at the theater in Foggia. On behalf of his mother, he thanked us for all our work, and gave an overall picture of how we, plus our luggage, would find our way home later that week. I was so impressed by his demeanor. I wondered if this was the first time he'd been sent on such a mission since his father's death. I assumed he'd been backstage in the Lido many times and had been accustomed to being amongst scantily clad girls, but still, he was only twenty-one. There he was, standing in our dressing room, looking very young, with twelve glamorous girls gathered around him while he talked. He didn't look terribly comfortable. He appeared shy and I thought would've preferred to be elsewhere, but he did what he came to do, and did it in a very poised manner. *Bravo!*

At last, we were on our way to Pescara, our last stop on the tour. Vera took a 6 a.m. train, much earlier than the rest of us, and took all our large suitcases with her. She had to register them at the luggage office in Pescara because they'd be transported to Paris as registered (unaccompanied) luggage.

Without Vera around, our train, leaving later that day, was a very happy train. It was a gorgeous day: the sky was blue, and we passed beautiful, deserted beaches. Everything was idyllic. Even Jack, the puppy, was happy, stretched out on the seat opposite to me.

While on the train I heard the news that very early that morning, Sandro and Giulia (with Anselmo driving) had raced the 120 miles to Pescara, as Giulia had gone into labor. When we arrived in Pescara, we got the good news that Giulia had given birth to a healthy baby girl. The quartet would be singing the final three shows without Giulia. That night, in their first number, Anselmo sang Giulia's part. That wasn't successful, so for the rest of the show they just left off her line in the music. In the final day's two performances, Wilma, an actress in the show, sang Giulia's part.

There were a few more last-minute things that had to be done before we headed for home. Gifts needed to be purchased for the dressers, an assignment that Deanna and I took on; and Annie and I headed out for some last-minute sunbathing on a beautiful beach just steps away from our hotel.

We had two shows on our final day. I was rather expecting a sad group of girls, dancing our numbers for the last time, but that wasn't the case. With the knowledge that we would never have to dance those numbers again, we danced our hearts out. It was a wonderful performance, one for the ages.

After the show the company came together for a final meal. We'd been family for nine months and it was all coming to an end. I knew I would probably never see any of these people again; for me it was a sad occasion.

The next morning the train for Paris left at 5 a.m. The Rome train left at 5:25 a.m. so those members of the company who were going to Rome came to see us off; that included Deanna and Kate, who were staying in Italy with Delio and Luciano. We Paris-bound travelers had a three-hour layover in Milan where we had lunch and did more last-minute shopping and then onward to Paris, with a beautiful ride through the Italian Lakes and Switzerland.

When we arrived in Paris, we'd been traveling for twenty-six hours. We were due to arrive at 7:25 a.m., but at 7 a.m. the train pulled into an unfamiliar station and all the passengers were told to get out. Miss Bluebell had sent her second son, Francis, to meet us with cash and tickets for our journey to London, but he was waiting for us at a different station. There was a rail strike going on in the city and we appeared to be stranded; so close to home, yet so far! We were so disappointed.

There were only five of us trying to get to London that day. Alice, Annie, Sophie, and Monica had taken Miss Bluebell up on her offer to see the show at the Lido that night, and Vera was staying on in Paris because she had to see Miss Bluebell. I would have loved to have seen the Lido show, but it would've meant the expense of a night's hotel in Paris, and another telegram to England, and also a disappointed family waiting with bated breath for my arrival. I couldn't do it.

Vera told us, in no uncertain terms, that it was impossible for us to get to England that day. She had a point. It was 7 a.m. and the boat train to Dieppe was scheduled to leave

Gare Saint-Lazare at 10 a.m. We didn't know if the boat train was even running, we didn't have French currency or tickets for the boat train and ferry; and our large suitcases still had to be collected from Customs. The odds were stacked against us!

We needed to get to Gare Saint-Lazare, from which the boat-train would leave, so some of us went to change lire to francs so we could hire porters for our many pieces of luggage, and others went to stand in the taxi line. There we hit a snag. Everyone on our train was in that line, and we estimated it would take us over an hour to reach the front. While we reconsidered our plan, Vera, who was making no attempt to help or advise us in our efforts to get to England, went off to Customs with our passports to pick up all the registered suitcases.

Sylvia noticed people getting on a bus and quickly found out (her French was good) that the bus was calling in at all the train stations. At that very moment Francis arrived, having responded to a phone call from Vera. (Because of the strike, he hadn't been expecting us to arrive in Paris at all that day, so hadn't been waiting for us at any of the stations.) Francis told us that Miss Bluebell wanted to see us at 1 p.m. We had different ideas and asked him to help us with our hand luggage onto the bus, and directed him to then stay put, and when Vera returned from Customs with the registered luggage, both of them should come to us at Gare Saint-Lazare, where we'd be waiting. Sylvia had also learned that there'd be a second bus later, and that was how they were to make the transfer.

Francis cooperated, and two-and-a-half hours later Vera and Francis arrived at Saint-Lazare, by which time the boat

ELIZABETH DALE PHILLIPS

train had already arrived and was sitting in the station. Francis immediately realized that he'd forgotten the tickets, so he called for some money which was to arrive in twenty minutes' time. Vera now saw another problem which made our travel "impossible." The Registration Office was closed therefore we couldn't transfer our large pieces of luggage directly through to Victoria Station. We quickly decided we'd handle the luggage ourselves. Not easy, but not impossible—we could do it.

Francis found a porter and all the luggage—and there was a lot—was loaded onto the train. Just then, Patrick, Miss Bluebell's older son, rushed up with money, lots of money, because Miss Bluebell had thought that more than five girls were making the trip. We were given money for the journey, and off we went.

In the general confusion of our departure, what with the immense amount of luggage and the late arrival of the cash, no one had asked to see our tickets, so we were not charged for our ride to Dieppe. We treated ourselves to porters for the entire journey, an expense normally covered by us, personally.

The train had only a few carriages, and there were very few people on the ferry, so in spite of being encumbered with much luggage, we had a great trip home and were treated like queens every inch of the way, with porters always at the ready and receiving excellent service during the meal. It was odd to eat English food once again; fish and chips and Cornish pasties, particularly as we now drank wine with it. After nine months in Italy, it seemed inconceivable to eat a meal without an accompanying glass of wine. All in all, it was a great way to finish the tour.

My brother, Michael, met me at Victoria Station. It was wonderful to see him, and I couldn't catch my breath, I was so emotional. He told me that he had a hard time identifying me when I got off the train: glamorous, blonde, and a bit thinner.

The goodbyes we girls exchanged were very brief. We were all busy, immersed in greeting our families or, if traveling onward, intent on finding porters. Whatever the reason, we were busy, and our goodbyes were probably too brief, considering how close we'd been for the past nine months.

Michael took me to his bedsitter for a cup of tea, and then, with his friend Chris, took me and my many suitcases to Euston station and put me on the train for Birmingham. I'd been traveling for forty hours, exerted a lot of energy hauling suitcases around railway stations, and I was weary.

Both my parents were at the Birmingham train station to meet me. We took a taxi home and sat up until 4 a.m., with me talking non-stop. I had a lot to say.

CHAPTER FIFTEEN

FINALISSIMO

And so, my life as a Bluebell came to an end.

I arrived in Canada five weeks later, where no one had ever heard of the Bluebell Girls, so I had to continue life as a mere mortal. I remained blonde for a few weeks and then went back to my normal hair color. My months of sleeping in hard rollers as required by Vera and pulling my hair tight every night into a chignon, had done their magic and my hair has remained pretty straight ever since, with just a useful amount of curl remaining. Vera had been right: you *can* straighten curly hair.

I'd developed some good habits in the Bluebells. Yes, there was a Captain to make sure it all happened, but it came down to each girl being the best she could be, every night, every performance. That's a good lesson to carry through life.

And another thing, after being accepted into the Bluebells and managing to survive rehearsals, even if there were humiliating moments, I'd learned that hard work pays off. It was a lesson I needed to learn, and a pity I hadn't learned it earlier. It's a lesson I absorbed and then incorporated into many activities in the ensuing years. It probably even helped me complete this book!

It would have been nice to have spent more time with the Bluebells, but life offers choices, and so often none of them are entirely right or wrong; and yes, I married Ian—and, yes, that's another story.

I'm now eighty-one and my life has continued to take twists and turns, just as it did in that Soho audition-room over sixty years ago—always landing me in a surprising new place, always in the midst of an abundance of rich new experiences. As I come to the end of this memoir, I realize how little I've changed. I'm still somewhat shy, I'm still thrifty, and still obey the rules (as long as they make sense). No, I really haven't changed.

And I still can't do the splits!

Photo credit: Kelly Spaine

ELIZABETH DALE PHILLIPS

Elizabeth lives with her husband, Bill, outside of Charlottesville, Virginia, close by the foothills of the Blue Ridge Mountains.

Born in England, she emigrated to Canada in her early twenties and moved to the States a few years later, settling in California. The next twenty years were spent raising two children and getting the education she'd so carefully avoided when she was a teenager.

With those endeavors behind her, her career options were either social work or accounting. She chose the latter and for the next twenty years worked as a financial auditor with the State of California.

Once retired, she devoted her time to music, the piano in particular, all styles of music, both solo and ensemble. She has since dabbled in the banjo and Scottish Dancing and became an enthusiast of Silver Swans and any exercise class that appeals to her.

Retirement was ticking along quite nicely when, after fifteen years, she dug out a hoard of letters she'd written many years earlier. Discovering that not only could she write, but she enjoyed it, she wrote a story about once upon a time when she was a dancer.

www.ingramcontent.com/pod-product-compliance
Lightning Source LLC
Chambersburg PA
CBHW020452100426
42813CB00031B/3338/J